"By introducing u. _____ , , _____ his writings, St. Thomas Aquinas rightly deserves his preeminence amongst the great theologians of the Church. But it is often forgotten that such greatness is the fruit of the humility necessary to stand before God, daily, in worship — at the Holy Sacrifice of the Mass and the Hours of the Divine Office. St. Thomas was a true *homo liturgicus* before he was a theologian, and his theology is the rich fruit of his liturgical roots, as Urban Hannon rightly underlines. At this critical time of the life of the Church, may St. Thomas's liturgical faith inspire us to return to Christ whom we encounter in a unique way in the Sacred Liturgy, so that we too may bring forth good fruit in due season!"

— **ROBERT CARDINAL SARAH**, Prefect Emeritus, Congregation for Divine Worship and Discipline of the Sacraments

"In this brief but profound study, Urban Hannon leads us to rediscover the lost art of medieval mystagogy as he shows the Church's greatest theological mind drawing forth the inexhaustible meanings of the Mass's words and actions, signs and mysteries. Clergy and laity alike will benefit from these pages, which are an incitement to reverence, praise, devotion, and contemplation."

— **SCOTT HAHN**, Franciscan University of Steubenville

"Thomas Aquinas as mystagogue? This will come as a surprise only to those who imagine Thomism as a kind of abstract religious philosophy. On the contrary, the ongoing rediscovery of St. Thomas as a complete and integral theologian, and consequently as a spiritual master, draws attention not only to the biblical and patristic roots of his thought, but also — as Urban Hannon's book successfully attests — to his deep theological insight into liturgical life, which is the ecclesial matrix of all Christian wisdom."

— **SERGE-THOMAS BONINO, O.P.**, Angelicum

"St. Thomas had much to say about the Mass — but one needs to know where to look. He did not write a stand-alone commentary; instead he made copious, scattered comments. Hannon is so steeped in the Master's multitudinous writings that he can wander through them, picking up tesserae with which to compose a mystagogical mosaic of the Mass. Thomas's voice rings out brilliantly and provocatively, yet we hear it thanks to Hannon, who provides a set of keys to unlock the symbolism of the ancient liturgy of the Mass."

— **DAVID W. FAGERBERG**, University of Notre Dame

THOMISTIC MYSTAGOGY

OS JUSTI STUDIES
IN CATHOLIC TRADITION
General Editor: Peter A. Kwasniewski

Thomistic Mystagogy

St. Thomas Aquinas's
Commentaries on the Mass

URBAN HANNON

Foreword by
Hugh Barbour, O. Praem.

Os Justi
Press

LINCOLN, NEBRASKA

Os Justi Press
P.O. Box 21814
Lincoln, NE 68542
www.osjustipress.com

Send inquiries to
info@osjustipress.com

ISBN 978-1-960711-62-5 (paperback)
ISBN 978-1-960711-63-2 (hardcover)
ISBN 978-1-960711-64-9 (ebook)

Typesetting by Michael Schrauzer
Cover design by Julian Kwasniewski
On the cover: Peter Paul Rubens (1577–1640),
The Defenders of the Eucharist, depicting
saints who played a pivotal role in
promoting and defending this mystery.

CONTENTS

FOREWORD

*The words of the wise are as goads, and as
nails deeply fastened in, which by the counsel of masters are given from one shepherd.
More than these, my son, require not. Of
the making of many books there is no end:
and much study is an affliction of the flesh.*
Ecclesiastes 12:11–12

EW ARE THE BOOKS
in any area of theological
inquiry of which we could
say that they were so sufficient as to render further searches unnecessary. Yet such as there are,
if and when we find them, are concise and illu-
minating, and one finds oneself saying, "Finally I
get it!" "I've never understood before as I do now."

These are the "goads," the "counsels of masters," given as though "by one shepherd," which
become as "nails deeply fastened" in our understanding. Only when we come across such works
do we understand how it is that "the making of
many books" and "much study" can be a merely

futile exercise and affliction. The boon we have received in insight simply disposes us to contemplate what we now possess in knowledge, and to cease from further restless precisions and amplifications which do not add to the intensive quality of our thinking, even if they may add a certain quantity of erudition.

The authors of such books are not the greatest masters themselves, but rather the keenest students of the greatest masters. They match their masters, not in the grand volume of their comprehensive writings, but in the lean precision of their appreciation. They are hard to list, since their authority is established in a very relative way, and there are always more waiting to be known.[1]

In fact, one may say without exaggeration that it is the task of every careful student to compose such lesser accounts of his greater masters' teaching in order to keep hold of the insights he has received from them — if nothing else, in a notebook of commonplaces, some file to which we add over time. This may be a happier reason than Qoheleth's for *faciendi libros nullus est finis*!

---

[1]   For theists and Christians generally one might name the Lewis of *Mere Christianity* or *The Abolition of Man*, and the Chesterton of *Orthodoxy*, and for Thomists, Pieper shines out, and Sertillanges, and Clerissac for ecclesiology, and for more recent students of the Mass there is the incomparable Joseph de Sainte Marie (Salleron), O. C. D., then for the understanding of prayer there is Gabriel Dieffenbach O. F. M. Cap.'s woefully little known gem *Common Mystic Prayer*, and for Mariology the suave treatise of De Koninck, *Ego Sapientia: The Wisdom That Is Mary.*

After all, are not the *Summae* of St. Thomas themselves, thanks to their very method, an ordering of such little, lesser, portable treatises woven together formally, reflecting architectonically how the whole of things comes forth and returns to its principle in sound judgment, while retaining the relation of each article in itself to the way in which we come to know, which is not the pattern of the whole, but that of our intelligence in motion? And thus the order of things and the order of coming to know are in their different ways reflected?

Regarding St. Thomas's teaching on the Eucharist, which is our interest here, Urban Hannon offers us the second half of a work not his own which needed to be completed. *Thomistic Mystagogy* is, I would have the reader understand, an unintended (to Urban) completion in precisely Thomistic terms, a kind of companion volume, to Dom Ansgar Vonier's *A Key to the Doctrine of the Eucharist*. Hannon would insist that Vonier would have done it better, but he didn't, and now surely is gratified from his place on high to favor the younger theologian's efforts.

The century which separates the publication of Hannon's work from the great abbot of Buckfast's only serves to illustrate the appositeness of this pairing. The key work of clarification of the sacramental sense of St. Thomas's eucharistic doctrine, and the demands this sense makes on

the consistency and rigor of its exposition and application, sets it apart from any positivistic or practical presentation. And yet it is just this sort of positivism which characterizes the preoccupation of the intervening liturgical movements, pre- and post-conciliar, and their approaches to the Mass. In the meantime, some Thomists are still content to entertain the French School rationales of the "essence" of the Mass as being found in the dispositions of the *soul* of the Incarnate Word, and not simply the offering of his body and blood!

So it is time to renew the forces of the greatest of eucharistic theologies by a return to Thomas pure and simple. Taking up Urban Hannon's *Thomistic Mystagogy* will provide Aquinas's attentive students with just that lively positive exposition which avoids the deadly positivism both of the ceremonial manuals of the pre-conciliar sort and of the bureaucratic "Office of Liturgy" *nomenklatura* authorities of the post-conciliar sort. What we need now is historical continuity with the liturgical sense of the Christian tradition — not a ruthless, historicist, "scientific" elimination of all allegory and subjective devotion, which is as foreign to the Epistle to the Hebrews as to Durandus or any of the medievals.

St. Thomas's understanding of the unique reality of the sacramental order is the exhilarating and demanding summit of his doctrine of the

Eucharist. This is Vonier's contribution. Thomas's devout exposition of the solemnities of the sacrament in the Mass is ours thanks to Hannon's present work, which is about the things which are "said and done around the sacrament," which are not its very being, but which nonetheless are not superfluous for its "being well." This is the kind of simple Thomistic language which overcomes a mere essentialist minimalism, for when would it ever in practice be interesting to separate a valued thing in its *esse* from its *bene esse*? One could never take away from the theology offered here an attitude which is accustomed to thinking, "Well, at least the Mass was valid!" And how many of us over the years, sadly, have said or thought something similar.

For this we can blame a certain kind of deracinated theology of the essence of the Mass, and a certain kind of liturgical theology. Let us have no more of either. A minimally valid Mass is an illicit and sacrilegious one. Canon law forbids as *nefas*, literally "unspeakable," the confection of the sacrament outside the *Missarum solemnia* even in extreme urgency. St. Thomas's eucharistic theology is not a matter of settling for less, just because we know what less is.

A final fraternal caution to fellow Thomists: Hannon is wise to point out as a faithful disciple, and not merely a fan of Aquinas, that Thomas is rarely novel in his ideas, and that his use of

others' opinions makes them no less his own. Too
often, in their zeal to justify the Angelic Doctor's
superiority, Thomists have looked for some new
insight or essentially "Thomistic" teaching, hith-
erto unknown. Here, however, in Thomas's mystagogical instructions, as in all his teaching on
sacramental and liturgical matters, we find only
a faithful recitation of what has been handed on
in the rite of the sacraments, and which might
easily have been written by almost any twelfth- or
thirteenth-century theologian. Nowhere is this
habit of his more evident than in his preferen-
tial and well-nigh exclusive use of the authority
of the Pseudo-Areopagite, whom he prefers to
call simply Dionysius, in matters which touch
on hierarchical worship, whether sacramental
or angelic. This attitude an all-pervasive one.[2]

---

2   In fact, throughout the works of St. Thomas, Dionysius is regarded as a supreme authority after sacred scripture and before the other Fathers in exegesis, theological
method, metaphysics, and angelology, as well as in liturgy
and spirituality. This, it is said, is because he is presumed
to be the earliest non-canonical writer, the convert of
St. Paul at Athens named in Acts 17. And yet it can hardly
be that an authority so developed, consistent, and universal could be based only on a simple historical error. The
content of his teaching, however historically recommended,
is beyond question. The Areopagite's teaching and the
Church's reception of it are undeniable and immoveable
facts of history and Christian theology. One need only
examine, for example, the acute use of the Areopagite in
medieval English vernacular literature on prayer to verify
its far-reaching influence. Of no one else did St. Thomas
say in the most absolute terms, and precisely regarding
the metaphysical principles of speculative thought, what

Thomas, would, it seems, have been ashamed
to be novel in expounding so great a mystery.
And this quality, perhaps, is what gives his twin
expositors, Vonier and Hannon, their own mea-
sure of humility and thus of a certain Thomistic
greatness. "May their words be as goads, and
as nails deeply fastened in," as they unite our
minds to the sacrament of the sacrifice offered
on the cross.

Fr. Hugh Barbour, O. Praem.
St. Michael's Abbey, California
January 1, 2024
Circumcision of Our Blessed Lord

---

he said of the Areopagite and his Christian Platonist disciples in his commentary *De Divinis Nominibus*: "*Verissima
est eorum opinio.*" One can only hope that Thomists will
begin to take his words *formalissime* as they were clearly
meant and draw fruitful conclusions therefrom! We await
a movement of Dionysian Thomists.

ACKNOWLEDGEMENTS

HIS BOOK BEGAN to take shape during my studies at the Angelicum—studies made possible by my dear friends John and Katherine Straus. My thanks are due to Fr. Thomas Joseph White, O.P., our rector magnificus, who first convinced me to come to Rome, then counseled me often once I arrived. In the fall of 2022, Fr. Dominic Jurczak, O.P., now the dean of theology, taught a licentiate course on St. Thomas and the liturgy; much of this book arose from discussions in his classroom, and so I owe a debt of gratitude both to him and to my classmates. The following semester, Fr. Cassian Derbes, O.P., gave me the opportunity to deepen my research in a independent study.

I was able to present sections of this book as lectures on six occasions: for the "Casathomists" at the Casa Santa Maria in Rome; at the Angelicum as a part of my lectio coram; on *The*

Josias Podcast; at the Pro Civitate Dei summer school in La Londe-les-Maures, France; for a group of Catholics in Stamford, Connecticut, organized by my dear friends Pedro José and Cristina Izquierdo; and at Ave Maria University for the conference "Thomas Aquinas and the Eucharist: Pathways to Revival." I appreciate the helpful comments I received on all of these occasions. I am especially thankful to Dominic Nalpon, whose enthusiasm for this project convinced me to make it available to a wider audience.

Jörgen Vijgen and Joey Belleza provided invaluable feedback on an earlier version of this study, as did two anonymous reviewers at *The Thomist*, who also convinced me that it would work better as a book than as a journal article. I am indebted to Fr. Andrew Hofer, O. P., for the observation that St. Thomas often cites liturgical texts under the name of St. Gregory the Great. Christopher Parrott shed light on some medieval terms of art, including "stole of the soul" and "second crucifixion." Benjamin Block helped clear up a manuscript discrepancy among *Summa* editions. Fr. John Wilson pointed me to a text on the Credo in the *Secunda Secundae* that I would otherwise have forgotten.

The Latin texts of St. Thomas, both those in the footnotes and those in Appendix 1, come from aquinas.cc. I am grateful to the Aquinas

Institute for making those so readily available. All translations into English are my own.

Peter Kwasniewski, my editor at Os Justi Press, brought this book from dream to reality. He has my special thanks for the diagrams in Appendix 2 (and for talking me out of the title *Thomystagogy*).

It is no exaggeration to say that Fr. Hugh Barbour, O. Praem., has taught me more about the holy Mass than anyone else I've ever known. I am honored that he agreed to write the Foreword.

Finally, I would like to thank my confreres in the Priestly Fraternity of St. Peter, especially those with whom I live at our international seminary in Wigratzbad, Germany. In addition to their encouragement for this little book, their daily love and care for the sacred liturgy created the ideal context in which to work on it. It is such a blessing to get to live among these mystical rites, the very object of St. Thomas Aquinas's contemplation.

THOMISTIC MYSTAGOGY

INTRODUCTION

HOMISTIC THEOL-
ogy is rarely associated
with liturgical prayer, even
by many of St. Thomas's own disciples. Such a
dissociation reveals more about the priorities
of later Thomism, however, than it does about
St. Thomas Aquinas, who himself devoted con-
siderable energy to the contemplation of the
sacred liturgy.[1] In fact, the longest question of

---

1 The relatively small group of recent and contem-
porary Thomists who have focused on St. Thomas Aquinas's liturgical writings includes: N. K. Rasmussen, Liam
Walsh, Franck Quoëx, David Berger, Joaquín Carmelo
Borobia Isasa, Antolín González Fuente, Innocent Smith,
and Dominic Jurczak. N. K. Rasmussen, "Saint Thomas
et les rites de la Messe: Étude historique sur la Somme
Théologique IIIa Pars, Q. 83, aa. 4 & 5" (unpublished
lectorate dissertation, Le Saulchoir, 1965). Liam G. Walsh,
"Liturgy in the Theology of St. Thomas," *The Thomist* 38
(1974): 557–83. Franck Quoëx, "Les actes exterieurs du
culte dans l'histoire du salut selon saint Thomas d'Aquin"
(unpublished doctoral dissertation, Angelicum, 2001);
"Les fondements anthropologiques du culte, selon saint
Thomas d'Aquin," *Sedes Sapientiae* 81 (2002): 49–82; "Le

the *Summa Theologiae* is about the meaning of the
Old Law's liturgical rituals.[2] The question of the
Summa with the most articles is the question on
prayer.[3] And no article in the *Summa Theologiae*
has more objections than the one about what can

---

culte dans l'ancienne alliance, selon saint Thomas d'Aquin,"
Sedes Sapientiae 82 (2002): 53–80; "Le Christ, religieux
de Dieu, selon saint Thomas d'Aquin," *Sedes Sapientiae*
83 (2003): 11–34; "Les sacrements, signes du culte divin,"
Sedes Sapientiae 86 (2003): 16–44; "Le sacrifice eucha-
ristique, sacrement de la passion du Christ selon saint
Thomas," *Sedes Sapientiae* 89 (2004): 13–42; "Thomas
d'Aquin, mystagogue: L'expositio missae de la Somme de
théologie (IIIa, q. 83, a. 4-5)," *Revue Thomiste* 105 (2005):
179–225, 435–72. Zachary Thomas has recently edited and
translated these various articles of Quoëx's into English.
See Franck Quoëx, *Liturgical Theology in Thomas Aquinas:
Sacrifice and Salvation History*, trans. Zachary J. Thomas
(Washington, DC: Catholic University of America Press,
2023). David Berger, *Thomas Aquinas and the Liturgy* (Ann
Arbor, MI: Sapientia Press, 2005). Joaquín Carmelo Boro-
bia Isasa, "La liturgia en la teología de santo Tomás de
Aquino" (unpublished doctoral dissertation, Toledo, Insti-
tuto Teológico San Ildefonso, 2009). Antolín González
Fuente, *Sacramentos, Liturgia y Teología En Santo Tomás
de Aquino* (Salamanca: Editorial San Esteban, 2012).
Innocent Smith, "In Collecta Dicitur: The Oration as a
Theological Authority for Thomas Aquinas" (STL thesis,
Washington, DC, Pontifical Faculty of the Immaculate
Conception, 2015); "Liturgical Prayer and the Theology of
Mercy in Thomas Aquinas and Pope Francis," *Theological
Studies* 79 (2018): 782–800; "1 Timothy 2, 1 and the
Expositiones Missae of Thomas Aquinas," *Sacris Erudiri*
58 (January 2019): 203–19; "St. Thomas Aquinas and
the Early Christian Virgin Martyrs," *Archivum Fratrum
Praedicatorum* 4 (2019): 5–36. Dominik Jurczak, *Cuestio-
nes litúrgicas en torno a santo Tomás de Aquino* (Valencia:
Cátedra Santo Tomás de Aquino, Facultad de Teología
San Vicente Ferrer, 2022).

   2　*ST* Ia-IIae, Q. 102.

   3　*ST* IIa-IIae, Q. 83.

go wrong in the celebration of holy Mass.[4] If we are to renew our liturgical formation through the "rediscovery of a theological understanding of the liturgy," therefore, then it is important for us to include the contribution of the theologian *par excellence*, the Common Doctor of Holy Church, St. Thomas Aquinas.[5]

The present study focuses on St. Thomas Aquinas's mystagogy of the Mass — that is, his theological teaching on the meaning and purpose of its various rites, for the sake of helping his fellow Christians better understand the mysteries they celebrate.[6] Unlike his teacher St. Albert the Great and many of their contemporaries, St. Thomas never wrote a stand-alone commentary on the eucharistic liturgy.[7] Nevertheless, and unbeknownst to many, St. Thomas

---

4 *ST* IIIa, Q. 83, a. 6.

5 Pope Francis, *Desiderio Desideravi*, 16.

6 For a few recent exercises in such mystagogy, granted not from a specifically Thomistic perspective, see David W. Fagerberg, *Liturgical Mysticism* (Steubenville, Ohio: Emmaus Academic, 2019); *Liturgical Dogmatics: How Catholic Beliefs Flow from Liturgical Prayer* (San Francisco, CA: Ignatius Press, 2021); *The Liturgical Cosmos: The World Through the Lens of the Liturgy* (Steubenville, Ohio: Emmaus Academic, 2023). See also Claude Barthe, *A Forest of Symbols: The Traditional Mass and Its Meaning*, trans. David J. Critchley (Brooklyn, NY: Angelico Press, 2023).

7 The Parma edition of St. Thomas's works (vol. 17) does include an *Expositio Missae Quid Significant Illa Quae Fiunt Ibi*, but we now know that this is simply an abbreviated version of the *Libellus de Canone Mystici Libaminis*, written by the twelfth-century Premonstratensian canon Richard of Weddinghausen.

did write his own *expositio Missae*. In fact, he
wrote two: one in his earliest major work, the
other in his latest. The former is hidden away in
the *expositio textus* of Book 4, Distinction 8, in
his *Scriptum* on the *Sentences* of Peter Lombard.
The latter is in the corpus of *Summa Theologiae*,
Tertia Pars, Question 83, Article 4. Both of these
treatments include a division of the liturgy into
its essential parts, as well as a detailed study of
the words that comprise each part — that is, "the
things said around this sacrament," the many
words of the whole Mass that surround the few
words of institution.[8] For although only that
barest form is necessary for the mere being of the
sacrament, all the words of the rite are necessary
for its well-being.[9]

Moreover, like every sacrament, the Mass signifies "in a twofold way, namely by words and
by deeds."[10] Thus both in the *Scriptum* and in
the *Summa*, St. Thomas supplements his commentary on the words of the Mass with a further

---

8 "ea quae circa hoc sacramentum dicuntur." *ST* IIIa,
Q. 83, a. 4, obj. 1. Here and throughout, all translations
of St. Thomas are my own.

9 "Ea quae pertinent ad solemnitatem sacramenti,
etsi non sint de necessitate sacramenti, non tamen sunt
superflua, quia sunt ad bene esse sacramenti." *ST* IIIa, Q.
66, a. 10, ad 4.

10 "In sacramentis aliquid dupliciter significatur, scilicet verbis et factis." *ST* IIIa, Q. 83, a. 5, c. See also the
parallel text in the *Scriptum*: "Sacerdos enim non solum
verbis, sed etiam factis, Christi passionem repraesentat."
In IV Sent., d. 12, ex. For a treatment of this principle
regarding the sacraments in general, see *ST* IIIa, Q. 60, a. 6.

reflection on its actions and gestures — that is, "the things done in celebration of this sacrament"[11] — and this specifically in the *expositio textus* of Distinction 12 of the same Book 4 of the *Sentences*, and in Article 5 of the same Question 83 of the *Tertia Pars*.

Drawing on all of these texts, and sensitive to their differences, this little book will try to piece together a properly Thomistic commentary on the Mass. By way of preparation, it will first consider how St. Thomas divides the Mass, the organization or order he finds within its structure; as well as according to its different speakers: priest, ministers, and choir; and finally according to the various significations of its elements. Following this *divisio Missae* in part 1, it will then present an *expositio Missae* in part 2, which will take the form of a running commentary on the rites of the Mass from beginning to end, integrating the various insights that are scattered across these four texts of St. Thomas: the two *expositiones textus* in the *Sentences*, and the two articles of the *Summa Theologiae*.[12]

---

11 "ea quae in celebratione huius sacramenti aguntur." *ST* IIIa, Q. 83, a. 5, obj. 1.

12 Very occasionally, for particular parts of the Mass, this study will also draw on other texts of St. Thomas. For one line in the Supplices Te Rogamus paragraph of the Roman Canon, for example, it will incorporate *In IV Sent.*, d. 13, ex. It will also return to this text when considering the name "Mass" as it relates to the Ite. For the Fraction Rite, in his *expositio textus* of Distinction 12, St. Thomas

"Because in this sacrament the whole mystery
of our salvation is embraced," St. Thomas says,
"thus it is carried out with greater solemnity." [13]
This is a study of that "greater solemnity," and
of how St. Thomas believes it relates to "the
whole mystery of our salvation." [14]

---

himself points back to his earlier treatment in Question 1,
Article 3, Quaestiuncula 3 of the same distinction — and so
this study will make use of that text as well. On one occasion, in connection with the Credo, it will also consider
the *Secunda Secundae*, namely *ST* IIa-IIae, Q. 1, a. 9, ad 6.

1 3   "Quia in hoc sacramento totum mysterium nostrae
salutis comprehenditur, ideo . . . cum maiori solemnitate
agitur." *ST* IIIa, Q. 83, a. 4, c.

1 4   This book will limit itself to a consideration of St.
Thomas himself, without investigating his various prede-
cessors and contemporaries. However, the fact that we will
not be trying to uncover St. Thomas's sources for each
of his mystagogical opinions should not be interpreted
to mean that he has no sources. St. Thomas is rarely an
altogether original thinker, nor is he trying to be. With
regard to the rites of the Mass, he takes his place in a
long lineage of *expositores Missae*. For the purposes of this
study, all that matters is that his writings express his own
judgments on these matters, regardless of whether he is
offering a new interpretation or repeating a mystagogical
commonplace. After all, St. Thomas's thoughts are no less
his own for having been learned from others.

I

Divisio Missae

HE TOOL OF *DIVI-sio textus* will be familiar to any reader of St. Thomas Aquinas's various commentaries, whether on scripture or Aristotle or anything else. Take, for example, his commentary on Psalm 1: "Therefore this psalm is divided into two parts. In the first, [X] is described. In the second, [Y] . . . . About the first, he does two things. First, [A] is treated; second, [B] . . . . In [the former], three things must be considered."[1] And so on. St. Thomas had learned from Aristotle that "it belongs to the wise man to order,"[2] and he applies that

---

1 "Dividitur ergo psalmus iste in partes duas. In prima describitur [X]. In secunda [Y] . . . . Circa primum duo facit. Primo tangitur [A]; secundo [B] . . . . In [A] tria consideranda sunt." *Super Psalmos*, Psalm 1, n. 1.

2 St. Thomas Aquinas, *SCG*, prooemium (paraphrasing Aristotle, *Metaphysics* I.2, 982a15-20).

lesson whenever he grapples with a new text. For St. Thomas, it is not enough to understand the various contents of a text, its matter, if one does not also understand the order of those contents, its form. The missal is no exception—although granted, when treating the Mass, Thomas is not primarily commenting on a book, but rather on the celebration itself, in word and in deed, which uses that book.

DIVISION ACCORDING TO STRUCTURE

In the *Sentences* commentary, St. Thomas begins his division of the Mass from the Dionysian exitus-reditus principle: "Because every operation of ours is begun by God, so it ought to be terminated in him, coming full circle. Thus the office of the Mass begins with prayer, and is terminated in thanksgiving."[3] St. Thomas then divides the Mass into three main sections,[4] the first of which corresponds to the aforementioned prayer or *exitus*, and the third to that thanksgiving or *reditus*, with everything in between making up the second, and by far the largest, part of the circle. He enumerates these three sections as follows: "[first,] the beginning of prayer which

---

3 "Quia omnis nostra operatio a Deo inchoata, circulariter in ipsum terminari debet; ideo Missae officium incipit ab oratione, et terminatur in gratiarum actione." *In IV Sent.*, d. 8, ex. See also Denys, *Celestial Hierarchy*, Chapter 1, 120B–121A.

4 "Unde tres habet partes principales." *In IV Sent.*, d. 8, ex.

lasts until [before] the Epistle; [second,] the celebration itself in the middle which lasts until [before] the Postcommunion; and [third,] the end of thanksgiving [which] then lasts from there until the end."[5]

Next St. Thomas subdivides the first main section in two: "The first part contains two things: namely the preparation of the people for prayer, and the prayer itself."[6] He then divides the former of these — that is, the preparation — into three: the Introit, the Kyrie, and the Gloria, according to three different ways that the people are prepared for prayer: "through devotion," through "humility," and "through right intention" respectively.[7] The prayer itself, which follows the preparation, of course refers to the Collect.

Thomas subdivides the second main section of the Mass, from the Epistle to before the Postcommunion, into three: "Yet the second principal part contains three parts. The first is the Instruction of the people until [before] the Offertory; the second, the Oblation of the

---

5 "principium orationis quod durat usque ad epistolam; medium celebrationem ipsam quae durat usque ad postcommunionem; et finem gratiarum actionis exinde usque in finem." *In IV Sent.*, d. 8, ex.

6 "Prima pars duo continet; scilicet populi praeparationem ad orationem, et ipsam orationem." *In IV Sent.*, d. 8, ex.

7 "Primo per devotionem," "Secundo humilitatem," "Tertio per rectam intentionem." *In IV Sent.*, d. 8, ex.

matter until [before] the Preface; the third, the consummation of the sacrament until [before] the Postcommunion."[8] The first of these three subdivisions, the Instruction, includes up to six things: the Old Testament readings, the Epistle, the Gradual, the Alleluia or Tract, the Gospel, and the Credo. Then the second of these three subdivisions, the Oblation, contains three things: the Offertory verse, the Oblation itself, and the Secret prayer. The third and last of these three subdivisions, the consummation, includes three things as well: the Preface, the Canon, and the rites for the reception of holy Communion. All of these elements of the second main section of the Mass could be further distinguished many times over. As we will see, for example, St. Thomas sees a careful order among the parts of the Roman Canon according to the tripartite distinction of *sacramentum tantum*, *res et sacramentum*, and *res tantum*. But let these details suffice for a first overview.

Finally, St. Thomas subdivides the third main section of the Mass into two: the Communion antiphon, and the Postcommunion prayer. Thus concludes the division of the Mass in St. Thomas Aquinas's *Scriptum* on the *Sentences*.

---

8 "Secunda autem pars principalis tres partes continet. Prima est populi instructio usque ad offertorium; secunda, materiae oblatio usque ad praefationem; tertia, sacramenti consummatio usque ad post communionem." *In IV Sent.*, d. 8, ex.

St. Thomas is less explicit about the plan
of the Mass in the *Summa Theologiae*, which is
perhaps to be expected given the difference in
genre. Unlike in the *Sentences*, he does not begin
his *Summa* commentary by drawing attention
to the exitus-reditus symmetry of the liturgy, or
indeed by calling out the main sections of the
Mass at all, and he uses fewer ordinal numbers
here as he works his way through the rites. Still,
a division of the Mass emerges. For the most
part, St. Thomas's two accounts of the order of
the Mass, in the *Sentences* and in the *Summa*,
harmonize quite well, especially considering
the nearly two decades that transpired between
them. Nevertheless, there are a few aspects of
the *divisio Missae* that are clearly different in the
Summa Theologiae.[9] For example, whereas in the
Sentences Thomas had grouped everything from
the Epistle through the reception of holy Communion under the heading of "the celebration
itself,"[10] in the *Summa* he does not recognize
the start of "the celebration of the mystery"[11]
until the Offertory, keeping the "Instruction of
the faithful"[12] separated off as its own distinct
part of the Mass — which would seem to be a

---

9 On the distinctions between St. Thomas's two
divisiones Missae, see Diagrams 1 and 2 in Appendix 2,
as well as Rasmussen, "Saint Thomas et les rites de la
Messe," 9–15.
10 "celebrationem ipsam." *In IV Sent.*, d. 8, ex.
11 "celebrationem mysterii." *ST* IIIa, Q. 83, a. 4, c.
12 "instructio fidelis populi." *ST* IIIa, Q. 83, a. 4, c.

fourth main part, if he were keeping count. [13]
Moreover, whereas before he had divided the
parts around the consecration according to the
sacramentum tantum, the *res et sacramentum*, and
the *res tantum*, now he foregoes that distinction,
while also adopting a new distinction between
"sacrifice" and "sacrament," the former of which
he has correspond to the Oblation, the latter
to the consecration and reception. [14] Despite
these small differences, St. Thomas is generally
consistent in his division of the Mass according
to its structure.

DIVISION ACCORDING TO SPEAKERS

He is also consistent in his division of the
Mass according to its speakers — that is, his
consideration of who says what, and why. For
"of those things that are said in the office of
the Mass, some are said by the priest, some by
the ministers, and some by the whole choir." [15]
St. Thomas believes it is fitting that the words of

---

13 This division into four also corresponds better to
the brief four-part *divisio Missae* that St. Thomas offers
in three other places in his corpus, according to the four
kinds of prayer in 1 Timothy 2:1: "obsecrationes, orationes,
postulationes, gratiarum actiones." See *In IV Sent.*, d. 15,
q. 4, a. 3; In *1 Tim 2*; and *ST* IIa-IIae, Q. 83, a. 17. See
also Smith, "1 Timothy 2, 1 and the *Expositiones Missae*
of Thomas Aquinas."

14 "Quod quidem et offertur ut sacrificium, et consecratur et sumitur ut sacramentum." *ST* IIIa, Q. 83, a. 4, c.

15 "Eorum quae in officio Missae dicuntur, quaedam
dicuntur per sacerdotem, quaedam per ministros, quaedam
a toto choro." *ST* IIIa, Q. 83, a. 4, c.

the Mass should be so distributed among these
three — priest, ministers, and choir — because
"things that pertain to the whole Church are mentioned . . . in this sacrament." [16] It is not enough
that the priest alone should speak, therefore, but
rather the whole hierarchy of the mystical body
ought to be represented through the speakers
of the Mass.

The priest himself is responsible for pro-
nouncing those words "by which the people is
immediately ordered to God," since the office of
priests is precisely to be "the mediators between
the people and God." [17] St. Thomas specifies
that these parts given over to the priest are "to
offer gifts and prayers for the people," which he
also connects with Hebrews 5:1: *For every high
priest chosen from among men is appointed to act
on behalf of men in relation to God, to offer gifts
and sacrifices for sins.* [18] Yet there is a distinction within the various things that the priest
says, since some are said "publicly," aloud for
all to hear, whereas others are said "privately"
or "secretly," in so quiet a whisper that they are

---

16 "In hoc sacramento . . . tanguntur ea quae pertinent ad totam Ecclesiam." *ST* IIIa, Q. 83, a. 4, ad 6.
17 "Ea quidem quibus populus immediate ordinatur ad Deum, per sacerdotes tantum dicuntur, qui sunt
mediatores inter populum et Deum." *In IV Sent.*, d. 8, ex.
18 "Quaedam vero sacerdos solus prosequitur, quae
scilicet ad proprium officium sacerdotis pertinent, ut scilicet dona et preces offerat pro populo, sicut dicitur Heb.
V." *ST* IIIa, Q. 83, a. 4, ad 6.

known to God alone.[19] St. Thomas finds that
the difference between these two kinds of enun-
ciation, public and private, is whether or not
the priest is "praying in the person of the people."[20] For some of the priest's words "pertain
both to the priest and to the people, like the
common orations" — and these are the things
he says publicly, out-loud, like the Collect and
the Postcommunion.[21] But others of the priest's
words "regard only the priest's own office, like
the consecrations and prayers of this sort that
he makes for the people, nevertheless not praying
in the person of the people" — and these are the
things he says privately, like the Oblation prayers
and the Roman Canon.[22] However, even these
silent parts of the Mass are made to include the
whole people. For whenever the priest is about

---

19 "Quorum quaedam dicuntur publice, . . . quaedam
privatim." *In IV Sent.*, d. 8, ex. "In his tamen quaedam
dicit publice, . . . quaedam vero . . . occulte a sacerdote
dicuntur." *ST* IIIa, Q. 83, a. 4, ad 6.

20 "in persona populi orans." *In IV Sent.*, d. 8, ex.

21 "In his tamen quaedam dicit publice, quae scilicet
pertinent et ad sacerdotem et ad populum, sicut sunt
orationes communes." *ST* IIIa, Q. 83, a. 4, ad 6. See also
In IV Sent., d. 8, ex: "Quorum quaedam dicuntur publice,
spectantia ad totum populum, in cujus persona ipse solus
ea Deo proponit, sicut orationes et gratiarum actiones."

22 "Quaedam privatim, quae ad officium ipsius tantum spectant, ut consecrationes et hujusmodi orationes
quas ipse pro populo facit, non tamen in persona populi
orans." *In IV Sent.*, d. 8, ex. See also *ST* IIIa, Q. 83, a. 4,
ad 6: "Quaedam vero pertinent ad solum sacerdotem,
sicut oblatio et consecratio. Et ideo quae circa haec sunt
dicenda occulte a sacerdote dicuntur."

to say anything, whether publicly or privately, he prefaces this with *Dominus vobiscum*, to get the people's attention and to turn their minds to God.[23] The people are, as it were, bookends to every prayer of the priest, since after each one as well, "the people consent, responding, *Amen*. Whence also," St. Thomas says, "every prayer of the priest is ended out-loud, even if it is said privately."[24] In the *Summa Theologiae*, Thomas also considers the possibility that perhaps the priest says some things secretly as a sign of the Passion, since the first priests were the apostles, and "around the time of Christ's Passion, the disciples confessed Christ only secretly."[25]

St. Thomas has the least to say about the words of the Mass pronounced by the lower ministers — namely the deacon, the subdeacon, and sometimes lectors as well, all of whom read at the Mass from the sacred scriptures. St. Thomas

---

23 "Et in omnibus praemittit: *Dominus vobiscum*, ut mens populi Deo conjungatur ad ipsum per intentionem erecti." *In IV Sent.*, d. 8, ex. "In utrisque tamen excitat attentionem populi, dicendo, dominus vobiscum . . . . Et ideo in his quae secreto dicuntur, publice praemittit, dominus vobiscum." *ST* IIIa, Q. 83, a. 4, ad 6.

24 "Et quia populus in his quae ad Deum sunt, sacerdotem ducem habet, ideo in fine cujuslibet orationis populus consentit respondens: *amen*; unde et omnis sacerdotis oratio alte terminatur, etiam si privatim fiat." *In IV Sent.*, d. 8, ex. See also *ST* IIIa, Q. 83, a. 4, ad 6: "Et expectat assensum dicentium, amen . . . . et subiungit, per omnia saecula saeculorum."

25 "Vel secrete aliqua sacerdos dicit in signum quod, circa Christi passionem, discipuli non nisi occulte Christum confitebantur." *ST* IIIa, Q. 83, a. 4, ad 6.

simply notes that their parts correspond to things that were first revealed through various ministers, namely the prophets, the apostles, and the inspired authors. In the *Sentences* commentary, St. Thomas says, "To those things that are handed down from above through the ministry of others, the people are ordered through the ministers of the altar."[26] Likewise in the *Summa*: "Some things are said through the ministers, such as the doctrine of the New and Old Testaments, as a sign that this doctrine was announced to the people through ministers sent by God."[27]

The last group responsible for some select words of the Mass is the choir. St. Thomas identifies their parts with "the things that pertain to the people," or "to the disposing of the people."[28] Now a further distinction is necessary, since some things the choir is responsible for in their entirety, like the Introit, Offertory, and Communion chants, whereas other things are first intoned by the priest and then completed by the choir together with the people, such as

---

[26] "Ad ea vero quae per ministerium aliorum divinitus sunt tradita, per ministros altaris populus ordinatur." *In IV Sent.*, d. 8, ex.

[27] "Quaedam vero dicuntur per ministros, sicut doctrina novi et veteris testamenti, in signum quod per ministros a Deo missos est haec doctrina populis nuntiata." *ST* IIIa, Q. 83, a. 4, ad 6.

[28] "Et ideo quaedam dicuntur a choro, quae pertinent ad populum." *ST* IIIa, Q. 83, a. 4, ad 6. "Ea vero quae ad dispositionem populi pertinent, chorus prosequitur." *In IV Sent.*, d. 8, ex.

the Gloria and the Credo.[29] St. Thomas distinguishes these according to whether the words express things "that exceed human reason" or things "that are consonant with reason."[30] In the case of those that go beyond reason, they are "intoned by the priest, who bears the person of God, as a sign that such things come to the people from divine revelation."[31] Here St. Thomas gives the examples of "faith and heavenly glory" — corresponding to the Credo and Gloria respectively.[32] Yet in the case of those things that do not require revelation, those "the choir says itself."[33] Furthermore, some things the choir says before those said by the priest or ministers, namely those that are "preparatory for receiving divine things," whereas others it says after, namely those that are "caused by the people's reception of divine things."[34]

---

29 "Quorum quaedam chorus totaliter prosequitur . . . . Quaedam vero populus prosequitur, sacerdote inchoante." *ST* IIIa, Q. 83, a. 4, ad 6.

30 "Quorum quaedam a sacerdote inchoantur, quae ad ea pertinent quae rationem humanam excedunt, quasi divinitus accepta: quaedam chorus per seipsum, quibus illa declarantur quae rationi sunt consona." *In IV Sent.*, d. 8, ex.

31 "Quaedam vero populus prosequitur, sacerdote inchoante, qui personam Dei gerit, in signum quod talia pervenerunt ad populum ex revelatione divina." *ST* IIIa, Q. 83, a. 4, ad 6.

32 "sicut fides et gloria caelestis. Et ideo sacerdos inchoat symbolum fidei et gloria in excelsis Deo." *ST* IIIa, Q. 83, a. 4, ad 6.

33 "quaedam chorus per seipsum." *In IV Sent.*, d. 8, ex.

34 "Item quaedam pertinent ad populum ut praeparatoria ad divina percipienda; et haec a choro praemittuntur

Of course, all of the above division of speakers pertains to the solemn high Mass, which St. Thomas takes as normative. Despite how much ink he spills on the rites of the Mass, St. Thomas speaks of the low Mass only once in these *expositiones Missae*, and only to defend its liceity.[35] Even there, he goes out of his way to recognize that the solemn Mass is preferable, quoting at length from a text of Pope Soter in Gratian's *Decretum*, and observing that at least bishops are commanded always to celebrate in the presence of many, for the sake of solemnity.[36] Nevertheless, St. Thomas recognizes that the Church does give a concession for low Masses: "In private Masses it suffices to have one minister, who bears the person of the whole Catholic people, in whose person he responds plurally to

---

his quae a ministris et sacerdote dicuntur; quaedam vero ex perceptione divinorum in populo causata; et haec sequuntur." *In IV Sent.*, d. 8, ex.

35 *ST* IIIa, Q. 83, a. 5, ad 12. St. Thomas does mention the low Mass offhandedly in the *Sentences* once as well, but not in the context of his *expositio Missae* there, and only to specify at what hours different kinds of Mass may be celebrated. See *In IV Sent.*, d. 13, q. 1, a. 2, qa. 4, c.

36 "In solemni celebratione Missae plures debent adesse. Unde Soter Papa dicit, ut habetur de Consecr., dist. I, *hoc quoque statutum est, ut nullus presbyterorum Missarum solemnia celebrare praesumat, nisi, duobus praesentibus sibique respondentibus, ipse tertius habeatur, quia, cum pluraliter ab eo dicitur, dominus vobiscum, et illud in secretis, orate pro me, apertissime convenit ut ipsi respondeatur salutationi.* Unde et, ad maiorem solemnitatem, ibidem statutum legitur quod episcopus cum pluribus Missarum solemnia peragat." *ST* IIIa, Q. 83, a. 5, ad 12.

the priest."[37] Such stripped-down Masses may
not be the ideal, but neither are they forbidden.

DIVISION ACCORDING TO
SIGNIFICATION

So much, then, for the division of the Mass
both according to its structure and according to
its speakers. If these divisions correspond to the
formal and (instrumental) agent causes of the
liturgy respectively, we conclude Part 1 with a
brief note on the liturgy's final cause, its end or
purpose. For St. Thomas, the words and actions
of the Mass come together for the sake of signifying three things: the representation of Christ's
Passion, the disposition of the Church, and the
devotion and reverence due to this sacrament.[38]
All three of these pertain, in different ways, to
the body of Christ. Beyond their signification,
the rites of the Mass are also for the sake of
divine worship. In fact, St. Thomas's entire

---

37 "In Missis tamen privatis sufficit unum habere
ministrum, qui gerit personam totius populi Catholici,
ex cuius persona sacerdoti pluraliter respondet." *ST* IIIa,
Q. 83, a. 5, ad 12.
38 "Significantur autem verbis in celebratione huius
sacramenti quaedam pertinentia ad passionem Christi,
quae repraesentatur in hoc sacramento; vel etiam ad corpus
mysticum, quod significatur in hoc sacramento; et quaedam
pertinentia ad usum sacramenti, qui debet esse cum devotione et reverentia. Et ideo in celebratione huius mysterii
quaedam aguntur ad repraesentandum passionem Christi;
vel etiam dispositionem corporis mystici; et quaedam
aguntur pertinentia ad devotionem et reverentiam usus
huius sacramenti." *ST* IIIa, Q. 83, a. 5, c.

expositio Missae in the *Sentences* commentary is
a gloss on a line from St. Ambrose, quoted by
Peter Lombard, and then again by St. Thomas:
"*Per reliqua autem omnia quae dicuntur, laus Deo
defertur.*" — "Through everything else that is
said" — the whole liturgy, that is, that surrounds
the words of institution — "praise is offered to
God."[39]

Therefore, with formal, agent, and final
causes accounted for, we proceed now, and for
the remainder of this book, to the matter of the
liturgy: the words and actions of which the Mass
is composed.

---

39 *In IV Sent.*, d. 8, ex.

II

Expositio Missae

HE FIRST MOMENT of the Mass mentioned by St. Thomas is the priest's Confiteor, his confession "before the Introit of the Mass," in which he begs to be purified through divine mercy.[1] In fact, it seems as though St. Thomas conceives of this Confiteor as taking place before the Mass proper has even begun, since he does not mention it in either of his running *expositiones Missae*, but only later in answer to an objection. This confession of the priest is necessary for the sake of the afore-mentioned devotion and reverence, St. Thomas says, for "such cleansing is required of him who approaches this sacrament."[2] The Confiteor is

---

1 "Quod etiam significatur per confessionem quae fit ante introitum Missae." *ST* IIIa, Q. 83, a. 5, ad 1.

2 "talis emundatio requiritur ab eo qui accedit ad hoc sacramentum." *ST* IIIa, Q. 83, a. 5, ad 1.

also the first time that the priest assumes a bowing position. Defending the reasonableness of the priest's bodily postures in general, St. Thomas argues, "Those things that the priest does in the Mass are not ridiculous gesticulations, for they are done to represent something."[3] About bows in particular, Thomas says, "The bows made by the priest signify Christ's obedience to the Father, out of which he endured death."[4]

PRAYER (INTROIT–COLLECT)

The first three moments of the Mass proper are the Introit, the Kyrie, and the Gloria, all of which are undertaken as preparation for the prayer of the Collect. Concerning these preparatory exercises, St. Thomas says, "Because it is written, *Guard your foot entering the house of the Lord* (Eccl 4:17), and, *Before prayer, prepare your soul* (Sir 18:23), thus before the celebration of this mystery, first of all there is a certain preparation for carrying out worthily the things that follow."[5]

---

3 "Ea quae sacerdos in Missa facit, non sunt ridiculosae gesticulationes, fiunt enim ad aliquid repraesentandum." *ST* IIIa, Q. 83, a. 5, ad 5.

4 "Inclinationes etiam factae a sacerdote, signant Christi obedientiam ad patrem, ex qua mortem sustinuit." *In IV Sent.*, d. 12, ex.

5 "Et quia scriptum est Eccle. IV, *custodi pedem tuum ingrediens domum domini*, et Eccli. XVIII, *ante orationem praepara animam tuam*, ideo ante celebrationem huius mysterii, primo quidem praemittitur praeparatio quaedam ad digne agenda ea quae sequuntur." *ST* IIIa, Q. 83, a. 4, c.

In the *Sentences*, St. Thomas characterizes the
Introit as a preparation "through devotion."[6]
This is why, he says, the text of the Introit is
taken from something pertaining to the feast or
occasion of this particular Mass, "in the devotion to which the people are gathered," in order
to excite their piety.[7] In the *Summa*, St. Thomas
similarly refers to this beginning of preparation
as a preparation through "divine praise."[8] Thus
he connects the Introit to Psalm 49:23: *A sacrifice of praise shall honor me, and there is the way by
which I shall show him God's salvation.*[9] It is fitting,
the Dionysian Aquinas believes, that the Introit
is usually taken from the Psalter — and that,
even when the Introit itself is not, it is at least
accompanied by a Psalm.[10] For as St. Thomas
has learned from the Areopagite, "The Psalms
embrace through the mode of praise everything
that is contained in sacred scripture."[11] The

---

6 "Primo per devotionem, quae excitatur in introitu."
In IV Sent., d. 8, ex.
7 "in cujus devotionem populus congregatur." *In IV
Sent.*, d. 8, ex.
8 "Cuius praeparationis prima pars est laus divina,
quae fit in introitu." *ST* IIIa, Q. 83, a. 4, c.
9 "secundum illud Psalmi, *sacrificium laudis honorificabit me, et illic iter quo ostendam illi salutare Dei.*" *ST* IIIa,
Q. 83, a. 4, c.
10 "Et sumitur hoc, ut pluries, de Psalmis, vel saltem
cum Psalmo cantatur." *ST* IIIa, Q. 83, a. 4, c.
11 "Psalmi comprehendunt per modum laudis
quidquid in sacra Scriptura continetur." *ST* IIIa, Q. 83,
a. 4, c. See also Denys, *Ecclesiastical Hierarchy*, Chapter
3, 429C–432A.

Introit, therefore, makes a doxological beginning to the overall worship of the Mass.

The Introit is followed by the Kyrie, an act of preparation through "humility." [12] According to St. Thomas, the Kyrie is sung for the sake of begging God's mercy — and since mercy is for the miserable, thus in the Kyrie "the one seeking mercy declares his misery." [13] St. Thomas offers a number of explanations for the ninefold character of this part of the Mass: three *Kyrie eleison's*, followed by three *Christe eleison's*, and then three more *Kyrie eleison's*. In the *Sentences*, he notices how this number corresponds to "the nine choirs of angels." [14] In the *Summa*, he considers the three sets of three as acting "against the threefold misery of ignorance, fault, and punishment." [15] But in both places, St. Thomas primarily associates the numerology of the Kyrie with the Most Blessed Trinity: "saying *Kyrie eleison* three times for the person of the Father; three times for the person

---

12 "humilitatem." *In IV Sent.*, d. 8, ex.

13 "misericordiam petens miseriam profitetur." *In IV Sent.*, d. 8, ex. See also *ST* IIIa, Q. 83, a. 4, c: "Secunda pars continet commemorationem praesentis miseriae, dum misericordia petitur." On mercy and misery in general, see *ST*, Ia, Q. 21, a. 3, c: "Misericors dicitur aliquis quasi habens miserum cor, quia scilicet afficitur ex miseria alterius per tristitiam, ac si esset eius propria miseria."

14 "Dicitur novies propter novem choros angelorum." *In IV Sent.*, d. 8, ex.

15 "contra triplicem miseriam ignorantiae, culpae et poenae." *ST* IIIa, Q. 83, a. 4, c.

of the Son, when *Christe eleison* is said; and
three times for the person of the Holy Spirit,
when *Kyrie eleison* is added."[16] St. Thomas sees
the threefold repetition of each as an allusion
to the doctrine of perichoresis or circuminces-
sion, namely that "all three persons are in one
another."[17] And so each of the three lines is
repeated three times, "according as each person is considered in himself and in order to
the other two."[18] Thus the nine lines of the
Kyrie consider in turn the Father in himself, the
Father in the Son, the Father in the Holy Spirit,
the Son in himself, the Son in the Father, the
Son in the Holy Spirit, the Holy Spirit in himself, the Holy Spirit in the Father, and the Holy
Spirit in the Son. The Kyrie is a plea for mercy
from this mutually interpenetrating Trinity of
divine persons.

The third and final preparation for the
Collect is the Gloria. It is fitting, St. Thomas
says, that this should follow the Kyrie, since
the Gloria "commemorates heavenly glory, to
which we tend after the present misery" which

---

16 "dicendo kyrie eleison ter pro persona patris; ter
pro persona filii, cum dicitur Christe eleison; et ter pro
persona spiritus sancti, cum subditur kyrie eleison." *ST*
IIIa, Q. 83, a. 4, c.

17 "vel ad significandum quod omnes personae sunt
in se invicem." *ST* IIIa, Q. 83, a. 4, c.

18 "vel propter fidem Trinitatis, secundum quod quaelibet persona in se consideratur et in ordine ad alias duas."
In IV Sent., d. 8, ex.

was commemorated by the Kyrie.[19] The Gloria is a preparation "through right intention, which must be directed to the heavenly fatherland and glory, which exceeds all human reason."[20] Nevertheless, unlike the Introit and the Kyrie, the Gloria is not said at every Mass, but only "on solemnities, which represent heavenly solemnity to us."[21] (Note that, for St. Thomas, "solemnity" seems not to be a particular rank of day, to be contrasted with "feast" or "memorial" or any other celebration, but rather just a generic term for all festal days in contrast to ferias.) The Gloria is especially to be omitted, St. Thomas says, "in offices of mourning, which pertain to the commemoration of misery" rather than of glory.[22] In terms of who is responsible for chanting this part of the Mass, the Gloria is an example of something "that the choir completes with the priest beginning

---

19 "Tertia autem pars commemorat caelestem gloriam, ad quam tendimus post praesentem miseriam, dicendo, gloria in excelsis Deo." *ST* IIIa, Q. 83, a. 4, c.

20 "Tertio per rectam intentionem, quae ad caelestem patriam et gloriam dirigenda est, quae omnem rationem humanam excedit; et hoc fit per *gloria in excelsis*." *In IV Sent.*, d. 8, ex.

21 "Et ideo non dicitur nisi in solemnitatibus quae nobis caelestem solemnitatem repraesentant." *In IV Sent.*, d. 8, ex. See also *ST* IIIa, Q. 83, a. 4, c: "Quae cantatur in festis, in quibus commemoratur caelestis gloria."

22 "Intermittitur autem in officiis luctuosis, quae ad commemorationem miseriae pertinent." *ST* IIIa, Q. 83, a. 4, c. See also *In IV Sent.*, d. 8, ex: "In officiis vero luctus omnino intermittitur."

it"[23]—which, again, means that it "pertains to those things that exceed human reason, as though received from above."[24]

The preparations of Introit, Kyrie, and Gloria having been completed, the people are ready at last for the Collect. St. Thomas describes this as "the prayer to God poured forth for the people," and as "the oration that the priest makes for the people, that they might be considered worthy of such great mysteries."[25] The priest prays the Collect publicly, introducing it with *Dominus vobiscum*, a formula that St. Thomas associates with Ruth 2:4.[26] However, if the Mass is being celebrated by a bishop and on a feast day, then the bishop substitutes *Pax vobis* for this *Dominus vobiscum*, because the bishop "[bears] the type of Christ, who addressed the disciples with these words after the Resurrection, in John 20:19."[27]

---

23 "Et hoc fit per *gloria in excelsis*, quam chorus prosequitur sacerdote inchoante." *In IV Sent.*, d. 8, ex.

24 "Quorum quaedam a sacerdote inchoantur, quae ad ea pertinent quae rationem humanam excedunt, quasi divinitus accepta." *In IV Sent.*, d. 8, ex.

25 "Deinde sequitur oratio ad Deum pro populo fusa." *In IV Sent.*, d. 8, ex. "Quarta autem pars continet orationem, quam sacerdos pro populo facit, ut digni habeantur tantis mysteriis." *ST* IIIa, Q. 83, a. 4, c.

26 "quam sacerdos publice proponit praemisso *Dominus vobiscum*, quod sumitur de Ruth 2." *In IV Sent.*, d. 8, ex.

27 "Pontifex autem dicit: *pax vobis*, gerens typum Christi qui his verbis discipulos post resurrectionem allocutus est, Joan. 20." *In IV Sent.*, d. 8, ex. See also *ST* IIIa, Q. 83, a. 5, ad 6: "Episcopus autem celebrans in festis in prima salutatione dicit, *pax vobis*, quod post resurrectionem dixit dominus, cuius personam repraesentat episcopus praecipue."

At this first *Dominus vobiscum* — or *Pax vobis*,
as the case may be — the celebrant also turns
himself around to face the people, something
that he will do five times in total over the
course of the Mass. St. Thomas believes that
these five turnings are symbolic of the Lord's
five post-Resurrection appearances on Easter
Sunday: "first to Mary Magdalene (John 20:14),
second to Peter (Luke 24:34), third to the
women (Matt 28:9), fourth to the disciples
going to Emmaus (Luke 24:15), fifth to the
disciples altogether (John 20:19)." [28] However,
the celebrant will greet the people like this a
total of seven times: the five times he turns
around, plus two when he does not — "namely
before the Preface when he says, *Dominus
vobiscum*, and [at the Pax] when he says, *Pax
Domini sit semper vobiscum*." [29] St. Thomas sees
these seven greetings as numerologically significant of "the septiform grace of the Holy
Spirit" — in other words, the Spirit's seven

28 "Quod autem quinquies se sacerdos ad populum
convertit, significat quod Dominus die resurrectionis quinquies se manifestavit: primo Mariae Magdalenae, Joan.
ult. secundo Petro, Luc. ult. tertio mulieribus, Matth. ult.
quarto discipulis in Emaus, Lucae ultim. quinto discipulis
in unum, Joan. ult." *In IV Sent.*, d. 12, ex. See also *ST* IIIa,
Q. 55, a. 3, obj. 3; and Q. 83, a. 5, ad 6.
29 "Salutat autem septies populum, scilicet quinque
vicibus quando se convertit ad populum, et bis quando se
non convertit, scilicet ante praefationem cum dicit, *dominus
vobiscum*, et cum dicit, *pax domini sit semper vobiscum*." *ST*
IIIa, Q. 83, a. 5, ad 6.

gifts.[30] Finally, in terms of the Collect itself, the priest prays with his hands lifted up, "to designate that his prayer for the people is directed to God."[31] St. Thomas finds scriptural warrants for this posture in Lamentations 3:41: *Let us lift up our hearts with our hands to God in heaven*; and in Exodus 17:11: *When Moses would lift up his hands, then Israel would be conquering.*[32]

CELEBRATION ITSELF
(READINGS–RECEPTION)

Inſtruction (Readings–Credo)

If everything before the Collect was preparatory for the Collect, the Collect itself is preparatory for what is to follow. The next stage of the Mass is what St. Thomas calls "the Instruction of the faithful people," which is important, he says, "because this sacrament is a mystery of faith."[33] This Instruction is accomplished

---

30 "Salutat autem populum septies ad septiformem gratiam Spiritus Sancti ostendendam. *Sine quibus mortalis vita duci non potest*; quia etsi possumus vitare singula, non tamen omnia." *In IV Sent.*, d. 12, ex. See also *ST* IIIa, Q. 83, a. 5, ad 6. On the seven gifts of the Holy Spirit in general, see *ST* Ia-IIae, Q. 68.

31 "Levat etiam manus orando, ad designandum quod oratio eius pro populo dirigitur ad Deum." *ST* IIIa, Q. 83, a. 5, ad 5.

32 "secundum illud Thren. III, *levemus corda nostra cum manibus ad Deum in caelum*. Et Exod. XVII dicitur quod, *cum levaret Moyses manus, vincebat Israel*." *ST* IIIa, Q. 83, a. 5, ad 5.

33 "Praemittitur instructio fidelis populi, quia hoc sacramentum est mysterium fidei." *ST* IIIa, Q. 83, a. 4, c.

"through the word of God" — that is, the sacred scriptures, which, as we have seen, are proclaimed not by the priest but by the ministers, since the word of God "came to the people from God through his ministers."[34] Yet there is a distinction here between different types of ministers, arranged in a hierarchy. For according to St. Thomas, "the ministry of the word of God is threefold."[35]

The first and lowliest kind of ministry is that of "prefiguration," which is the ministry of the word of God that is active in the Old Testament.[36] At the Mass, therefore, such Old Testament readings are done by "inferior ministers," namely "lectors."[37] However, not every Mass includes these extra lessons from the Old Testament. St. Thomas identifies the Masses that

---

34 "Instructio autem populi fit per verbum Dei, quod quidem a Deo per ministros suos ad populum pervenit; et ideo ea quae ad instructionem plebis pertinent, non dicuntur a sacerdote, sed a ministris." *In IV Sent.*, d. 8, ex.

35 "Ministerium autem verbi Dei est triplex." *In IV Sent.*, d. 8, ex.

36 "Tertium figurationis, quod competit praedicatoribus veteris testamenti." *In IV Sent.*, d. 8, ex. It should be noted that, in the *Sentences* commentary, St. Thomas treats these in the reverse order, so that he can treat Christ himself first, who is the principle of the other two. For the sake of clarity, I have chosen to adopt the order of the *Summa Theologiae*, since this is also the chronological order of the Mass.

37 "Doctrina vero praedicatorum veteris testamenti per inferiores ministros legitur." *In IV Sent.*, d. 8, ex. "Quae quidem instructio dispositive quidem fit per doctrinam prophetarum, . . . quae in Ecclesia legitur per lectores." *ST* IIIa, Q. 83, a. 4, c.

do have such lessons as "those days when the configuration of the New and Old Testaments is especially indicated, such as on the Ember Day fasts" — as well as days "when various things are celebrated that are prefigured in the Old Law, like the Passion, the Nativity, the Baptism, and whatever else of this sort."[38]

The second ministry of the word of God is that of "manifest truth," which is proper to the preachers of the New Testament.[39] This pertains to the subdeacon's proclamation of the Epistle lesson — a generic name that also covers Acts and Revelation, effectively anything from the New Testament except the Gospels.[40] Occasionally, the subdeacon even reads something from the Old Testament here in place of the Epistle — which is different than the extra Old Testament readings done by lectors which were mentioned above. St. Thomas says that having the subdeacon sometimes read from the Old Testament instead of the New is entirely

---

38 "non semper, sed illis diebus quibus praecipue configuratio novi et veteris testamenti designatur, ut in jejuniis quatuor temporum, et quando aliqua celebrantur quae in veteri lege figurata sunt, sicut passio, nativitas, baptismus, et aliquod hujusmodi." *In IV Sent.*, d. 8, ex.

39 "Secundum manifestae veritatis quae competit praedicatoribus novi testamenti, de quo dicitur 2 Corinth. 3, 6: *qui et idoneos nos fecit ministros*, etc." *In IV Sent.*, d. 8, ex.

40 "Doctrina vero praedicatorum novi testamenti proponitur per subdiaconos." *In IV Sent.*, d. 8, ex. See also *ST* IIIa, Q. 83, a. 4, c: "Quae quidem instructio dispositive quidem fit per doctrinam . . . apostolorum, quae in Ecclesia legitur per . . . subdiacones."

appropriate, "because the preachers of the New Testament also preach the Old" — an application of the general principle about potential parts, namely that the power to do the greater includes the power to do the lesser.[41]

St. Thomas characterizes both whatever Old Testament lessons as well as the Epistle lesson as instructing the people "dispositively" — disposing them, that is, for the teaching of Christ himself.[42] Before we encounter Christ's own teaching in the Gospel, however, first we must consider the things that come before this final scripture lesson of the Mass, namely the Gradual and the Alleluia. According to St. Thomas, the dispositive readings of the Old and New Testament produce a twofold effect in the faithful. The first is progress in the moral life, "an advancement of the virtues," and this is signified by the Gradual.[43] The Gradual takes its name from *gradus*, meaning "step" or "stair," which, in this context, has both a literal and a symbolic meaning. Literally, the Gradual is named for the steps of the altar, since that is

---

41 "Nec obstat quod aliquando ab eis legitur loco epistolae aliquid de veteri testamento, quia praedicatores novi testamenti etiam vetus praedicant." *In IV Sent.*, d. 8, ex. On potential parts, see *In II Sent.*, d. 9, q. 1, a. 3, ad 1.

42 "dispositive." *ST* IIIa, Q. 83, a. 4, c.

43 "Ex doctrina autem ordinante ad Christum duplex effectus populo provenit: . . . scilicet profectus virtutum, qui per graduale insinuatur." *In IV Sent.*, d. 8, ex. See also *ST* IIIa, Q. 83, a. 4, c: "Post quam lectionem, cantatur a choro graduale, quod significat profectum vitae."

where the Gradual is said.[44] Symbolically, it is named for "the step by which one ascends from virtue to virtue."[45] The Old Testament and Epistle lessons cause this moral ascent, and this ascent in turn becomes, along with the lessons that caused it, another disposition toward the perfect teaching of Christ.[46]

The second effect of the earlier scripture lessons is a kind of eschatological rejoicing, "the exultation that comes from the hope of eternal things," and this is signified by the Alleluia.[47] Yet unlike the Gradual which is sung straight through, St. Thomas observes that the Alleluia is repeated. He explains that this repetition is on account of what he calls "the stole of the soul and the stole of the body" — that is, the perfect beatitude that comes from enjoying the beatific vision even before the resurrection of the body (the stole of the soul), and then the full flowering of that beatitude when the body too is raised in glory (the stole of the body).[48]

---

44 "vel a gradibus altaris ante quos dicitur." *In IV Sent.*, d. 8, ex.

45 "Dicitur enim a gradu quo ascenditur de virtute in virtutem." *In IV Sent.*, d. 8, ex.

46 "quibus etiam homo praeparatur ad doctrinam Christi" *In IV Sent.*, d. 8, ex.

47 "et exultatio habita de aeternorum spe, quod insinuat *alleluja*." *In IV Sent.*, d. 8, ex. See also *ST* IIIa, Q. 83, a. 4, c: "et alleluia, quod significat spiritualem exultationem . . . . Haec enim consequi debent in populo ex praedicta doctrina."

48 "Unde et replicatur propter stolam animae et corporis." *In IV Sent.*, d. 8, ex. See also *Super Matthaeum* 25,

Thus the Alleluia always looks forward to heaven with joy. This is especially true in the Easter season, when an extra Alleluia replaces the Gradual. According to St. Thomas, these Paschaltide Alleluias are "on account of the joy of the Resurrection," and it is a double Alleluia to signify the resurrection both "of the head and of the members."[49] However, at the other extreme from the double Alleluias of Easter, there are also Masses without any Alleluia at all, namely "on days and in offices of mourning," when such joy would not be appropriate.[50] In place of the Alleluia, these sorrowful liturgies substitute a Tract, which, St. Thomas says, "signifies spiritual groaning."[51] To Thomas, the Tract "suggests the exile of present misery," an effect it achieves "by the harshness of its voices and the prolixity of its words."[52] The Tract is long, in other words, and not especially melodious.

---

l. 3: "Notandum quod praemium quod iusto Dei iudicio datur hominibus, est duplex: primum est stola animae, et secundum stola corporis. Quantum ad stolam animae, in morte recipitur, sed tunc gloriam corporis simul recipient."

49 "Tempore autem resurrectionis duplex *alleluja* dicitur propter gaudium resurrectionis capitis, et membrorum." *In IV Sent.*, d. 8, ex.

50 "In diebus vero et officiis luctus intermittitur." *In IV Sent.*, d. 8, ex. See also *ST* IIIa, Q. 83, a. 4, c: "vel tractus, in officiis luctuosis."

51 "qui significat spiritualem gemitum." *ST* IIIa, Q. 83, a. 4, c.

52 "Loco ejus, tractus ponitur, qui asperitate vocum et prolixitate verborum praesentis miseriae incolatum insinuat." *In IV Sent.*, d. 8, ex.

After the Gradual and the Alleluia, or the double Alleluia, or the Gradual and the Tract, at last the rites of the Mass arrive at Christ's own instruction, the Gospel. Whereas the Old Testament reading had corresponded to the ministry of "prefiguration," and the Epistle reading to that of "manifest truth," the Gospel shows forth the ministry of "authority" — namely of Christ himself, whom St. Paul refers to as *minister* in Romans 15:8, and whom St. Matthew describes as *teaching in power* in Matthew 7:29.[53] Whereas the people were instructed only "dispositively" by those earlier lessons, now they are instructed "perfectly."[54] Therefore, whereas the dispositive lessons were sung by the lectors and subdeacon, the perfect lesson of the Gospel is chanted by the deacon, who is the highest of the liturgical ministers.[55] It is also noteworthy that the dialogue before the Gospel is the only time that the words *Dominus vobiscum* are

53 "Ministerium autem verbi Dei est triplex. Primum auctoritatis, quod competit Christo qui dicitur *minister*, Rom. 15, de quo dicitur Matth. 7, 29: *erat autem in potestate docens*. Secundum manifestae veritatis quae competit praedicatoribus novi testamenti, de quo dicitur 2 Corinth. 3, 6: *qui et idoneos nos fecit ministros*, etc. Tertium figurationis, quod competit praedicatoribus veteris testamenti." *In IV Sent.*, d. 8, ex.

54 "dispositive . . . perfecte." *ST* IIIa, Q. 83, a. 4, c.

55 "Perfecte autem populus instruitur per doctrinam Christi in Evangelio contentam, quae a summis ministris legitur, scilicet a diaconibus." *ST* IIIa, Q. 83, a. 4, c. See also *In IV Sent.*, d. 8, ex: "Et ideo doctrinam Christi proponit diaconus."

given to anyone but the priest: "Because Christ is not only man but also God," thus the deacon sings this greeting before the Gospel, "so that he might make men attentive to Christ as God." [56] Finally, St. Thomas comments on how fitting it is that the Gospel should come last among the scriptural lessons of the Mass, even though the Gospels precede the Epistles in the organization of the canon, and even though the events of Christ's earthly life recounted in the Gospels precede and are presupposed to the rest of the New Testament. "Because both of these teachings are ordered to Christ," St. Thomas says, "both the teaching of those who went before him [in the Old Testament], and that of those who followed after him [in the New Testament], thus the teaching of Christ is proclaimed at the end." [57] The arrangement is neither canonical nor chronological, therefore, but teleological: The Gospels come last in the Mass because everything else in scripture is for their sake. This concludes St. Thomas's discussion of the lessons from the word of God.

The Instruction, however, is not over just yet. There is one final element of this section of

---

56 "Et quia Christus non solum est homo, sed Deus; ideo diaconus praemittit: *Dominus vobiscum*, ut ad Christum quasi ad Deum homines attentos faciat." *In IV Sent.*, d. 8, ex.

57 "Et quia utraque doctrina ordinat ad Christum, et eorum qui praeibant, et eorum qui sequebantur; ideo doctrina Christi postponitur quasi finis." *In IV Sent.*, d. 8, ex.

the Mass, at least at some Masses, namely the
Credo. In the *Sentences* commentary, St. Thomas
explains that the Credo follows naturally from
the Gospel inasmuch as "the effect of the Gospel teaching is the confession of faith." [58] In
the *Tertia Pars*, Thomas elaborates on this reason: It is precisely because "we believe Christ
as divine truth" that, after the Gospel is read,
"the Symbol of faith is sung, in which the people show that they assent through faith to the
doctrine of Christ" contained in the Gospel. [59]
In his treatment of faith in the *Secunda Secundae*, St. Thomas remarks on how fitting it is
that it is precisely the Nicene Creed which is
sung at Mass, whereas the Apostles Creed is
recited silently at Prime and Compline, since
the Apostles Creed was composed when the
faith was still in hiding, but the Nicene Creed,
which is the Fathers' explanation of the Apostles Creed, was composed after the faith was
made public, and so it ought to be proclaimed
publicly in the Church's liturgy. [60] As far as why

---

58 "Effectus autem evangelicae doctrinae est fidei
confessio." *In IV Sent.*, d. 8, ex.

59 "Et quia Christo credimus tanquam divinae veritati,
secundum illud Ioan. VIII, *si veritatem dico vobis, quare vos
non creditis mihi?*, Lecto Evangelio, symbolum fidei cantatur,
in quo populus ostendit se per fidem doctrinae Christi
assentire." *ST* IIIa, Q. 83, a. 4, c.

60 "Quia symbolum patrum est declarativum symboli
apostolorum, et etiam fuit conditum fide iam manifestata
et Ecclesia pacem habente, propter hoc publice in Missa
cantatur. Symbolum autem apostolorum, quod tempore

the Credo is included in some Masses and not
in others, St. Thomas says that it is reserved
for the solemnities that are mentioned in the
Credo itself—for example: Christmas (*Et incar-
natus est de Spiritu Sancto ex Maria Virgine, et
homo factus est*), and Easter (*Et resurrexit tertia
die, secundum Scripturas*), and indeed any feast
of our Lord or of our Lady, both of whom are
named in the Credo, as well as the feasts of the
apostles, since the Credo is the Symbol of the
faith and the apostles are counted as "founders
of the faith."[61] Like with the Gloria, the Credo
is intoned by the priest and completed by the
choir, to show that it pertains to the whole
people, but also that the truths it contains are
above human reason.[62]

Oblation (*Offertory Antiphon–Secret*)

The next stage of the Mass is the Offertory,
which St. Thomas usually generically refers to as

---

persecutionis editum fuit, fide nondum publicata, occulte
dicitur in prima et in completorio, quasi contra tenebras
errorum praeteritorum et futurorum." *ST* IIa-IIae, Q. 1,
a. 9, ad 6.

61 "Nec dicitur nisi in illis solemnitatibus de quibus
fit mentio in symbolo, sicut de nativitate, resurrectione,
de apostolis, qui fidei fundatores extiterunt, ut dicitur 1
Corinth. 3, 10: *ut sapiens architectus fundamentum posui.*" *In
IV Sent.*, d. 8, ex. "Cantatur autem hoc symbolum in festis
de quibus fit aliqua mentio in hoc symbolo, sicut in festis
Christi et beatae virginis, et apostolorum, qui hanc fidem
fundaverunt, et in aliis huiusmodi." *ST* IIIa, Q. 83, a. 4, c.

62 "Quia supra rationem est, a sacerdote inchoatur
symbolum fidei et chorus prosequitur." *In IV Sent.*, d. 8, ex.

the Oblation. The *Sentences* commentary divides this into three: the Offertory antiphon, the Oblation proper, and the Secret.[63] The *Summa* treats this part of the Mass much more quickly, and does not explicitly distinguish the Oblation and the Secret, since both of these are said by the priest, in contradistinction to the Offertory verse that is chanted by the choir.[64] St. Thomas remarks that all of these — the Offertory antiphon, the Oblation, and the Secret — "require the lifting up of the mind to God," and thus they are preceded all together by a *Dominus vobiscum*.[65]

Among these three, the Offertory verse comes first, and it is intended "as preparatory" for what is to follow, namely the offering of the priest.[66] Like everything sung by the choir, this Offertory verse pertains to the whole people. Indeed, St. Thomas describes the Offertory as the *"laus populi"* — "the praise of the people."[67] In particular, this antiphon signifies the "exultation of those offering," their "happiness"

63 "Deinde sequitur secunda pars partis secundae principalis quae pertinet ad materiae consecrandae oblationem; et hic tria continentur." *In IV Sent.*, d. 8, ex.

64 "Circa oblationem vero duo aguntur, scilicet laus populi, in cantu offertorii, per quod significatur laetitia offerentium." *ST* IIIa, Q. 83, a. 4, c.

65 "Et quia haec tria praedicta exigunt mentis erectionem ad Deum, ideo omnibus tribus praemittitur: *Dominus vobiscum*." *In IV Sent.*, d. 8, ex.

66 "Praemittitur enim offerentium exultatio, quasi praeparatoria, in offertorio." *In IV Sent.*, d. 8, ex.

67 *ST* IIIa, Q. 83, a. 4, c.

in this moment, namely about the offering the priest will make on their behalf.[68] Thus St. Thomas connects this Offertory verse with 2 Corinthians 9:7: *God loves a cheerful giver.*[69]

St. Thomas has very little to say about the Oblation itself — only that it is expressed by the priest's prayer *Suscipe sancta Trinitas.*[70] Thomas also notes that both of the aforementioned elements, namely the joyful Offertory verse of the choir and the offering itself of the priest, are reflected in the Old Testament oblations of King David.[71]

There follows the Secret prayer, which is prepared for in two ways. As regards the priest, he prepares himself through humiliation, by the prayer *In spiritu humilitatis et in animo contrito suscipiamur a te, Domine.*[72] As regards the people, the priest prepares them through the *Orate fratres*, which functions like a *Dominus vobiscum*, alerting them that he is about to offer this

68 "offerentium exultatio." *In IV Sent.*, d. 8, ex. "laetitia offerentium." *ST* IIIa, Q. 83, a. 4, c.

69 "in offertorio, quia *hilarem datorem diligit Deus*, 2 Corinth. 9, 7." *In IV Sent.*, d. 8, ex.

70 "Exprimitur ipsa oblatio dum dicitur: *suscipe sancta Trinitas.*" *In IV Sent.*, d. 8, ex.

71 "Unde, I Paralip., dixit David, *ego in simplicitate cordis mei obtuli universa haec, et populum tuum qui hic repertus est, vidi cum ingenti gaudio tibi offerre donaria*, et postea orat, dicens, *domine Deus, custodi hanc voluntatem.*" *ST* IIIa, Q. 83, a. 4, c.

72 "ad quam orationem sacerdos per humiliationem se praeparat dicens: *in spiritu humilitatis et in animo contrito suscipiamur a te Domine.*" *In IV Sent.*, d. 8, ex.

prayer and so raising their minds to God.[73] In the Secret itself, the priest begs God to accept this Oblation that he, the priest, has made.[74] St. Thomas notes that is fitting that this should be said secretly — hence its name — "because it belongs to the priest alone to placate God with oblations."[75]

In addition to these various words surrounding the Oblation, this part of the Mass also contains two significant actions: the incensations, and the Lavabo.[76] Like many elements of the eucharistic liturgy, both of these have parallels in the ceremonial precepts of the Old Covenant as well, in which Aaron was commanded both to burn incense upon the altar, and to be ritually washed before offering sacrifice. Nevertheless, St. Thomas teaches, neither of these practices is included in the Mass as a carry-over from the Old Testament, as though Christians were

---

73 "*Dominus vobiscum*, loco cujus quando oratio secreta facienda est, dicitur: *orate fratres.*" *In IV Sent.*, d. 8, ex.

74 "Exprimitur ipsa oblatio dum dicitur: *suscipe sancta Trinitas*: petitur oblationis acceptatio per orationes secreto dictas." *In IV Sent.*, d. 8, ex. See also *ST* IIIa, Q. 83, a. 4, c: "oratio sacerdotis, qui petit ut oblatio populi sit Deo accepta."

75 "quia hoc sacerdotis tantum est Deum oblationibus placare." *In IV Sent.*, d. 8, ex.

76 Of course, this is not the first time during the Mass that incense would have been used, but I have waited to treat it until now because this is the most elaborate and extensive use of incense in the Mass, and because St. Thomas treats it together with the washing of the priest's hands.

still bound to obey the Old Law's regulations for worship — "but rather," St. Thomas says, "as instituted by the Church," and "as something fitting in itself."[77] Thus our use of incense differs from that of the ancient Jews, whose ceremonial laws have been abrogated.[78] In the context of the Mass, St. Thomas identifies two purposes for incense. The first pertains to reverence for the sacrament, and here his thought is eminently practical: The priest imposes incense "so that, if there were any trace of a bad odor bodily in the place that could provoke disgust, it might be dispelled through a good odor."[79] The second purpose is more spiritual: The incense represents "the effect of grace," since Christ was full of grace, as though of a good odor.[80] But this full grace of Christ is diffused to all the faithful through the actions of his ministers. Therefore, St. Thomas says, "once the altar has

77 "Nec tamen Ecclesia hoc servat tanquam caeremoniale veteris legis praeceptum, sed quasi ab Ecclesia institutum, sicut quiddam secundum se conveniens." *ST* IIIa, Q. 83, a. 5, ad 1.

78 "Unde non eodem modo utimur sicut in veteri lege erat statutum." *ST* IIIa, Q. 83, a. 5, ad 2. On the abrogation of the Old Testament ceremonial laws, see *ST* Ia-IIae, Q. 103, a. 3.

79 "Primo quidem, ad reverentiam huius sacramenti, ut scilicet per bonum odorem depellatur si quid corporaliter pravi odoris in loco fuerit, quod posset provocare horrorem." *ST* IIIa, Q. 83, a. 5, ad 2.

80 "Secundo, pertinet ad repraesentandum effectum gratiae, qua, sicut bono odore, Christus plenus fuit, secundum illud Gen. XXVII, *ecce, odor filii mei sicut odor agri pleni.*" *ST* IIIa, Q. 83, a. 5, ad 2.

been incensed everywhere, through which altar Christ is designated, all are incensed according to their order."[81] Thus the incense at Mass shows forth the sanctity of Christ, the sweetness of his grace, the function of his ministers, and the hierarchy of his Church.

The Lavabo — that is, the *"ablutio manuum"* or washing of the priest's hands — is likewise done "out of reverence for this sacrament."[82] Once again, this has both a practical purpose and a symbolic purpose. The practical purpose, pertaining to the body, is that we never handle precious things without washing our hands first.[83] "Whence it seems indecent," St. Thomas says, "that anyone should approach so great a sacrament with hands that are, even bodily, unwashed."[84] The symbolic purpose, pertaining to the soul, is that "the washing of the extremities signifies the cleansing from even the smallest of sins."[85] Here St. Thomas cites

---

81 "Et a Christo derivatur ad fideles officio ministrorum, secundum illud II Cor. II, *odorem notitiae suae spargit per nos in omni loco.* Et ideo, undique thurificato altari, per quod Christus designatur, thurificantur omnes per ordinem." *ST* IIIa, Q. 83, a. 5, ad 2.

82 "ablutio manuum fit in celebratione Missae propter reverentiam huius sacramenti." *ST* IIIa, Q. 83, a. 5, ad 1.

83 "Primo quidem, quia aliqua pretiosa tractare non consuevimus nisi manibus ablutis." *ST* IIIa, Q. 83, a. 5, ad 1.

84 "Unde indecens videtur quod ad tantum sacramentum aliquis accedat manibus, etiam corporaliter, inquinatis." *ST* IIIa, Q. 83, a. 5, ad 1.

85 "extremitatum ablutio significat emundationem etiam a minimis peccatis." *ST* IIIa, Q. 83, a. 5, ad 1.

both the Dionysian *Ecclesiastical Hierarchy*, as
well as Christ's words at the Last Supper about
the necessity for those who have bathed to be
washed.[86] St. Thomas also connects the Lavabo
to the priest's Confiteor before the Introit, since
both of these are for the sake of being cleansed
before offering sacrifice.[87] As with the incensations, St. Thomas insists that, despite the Old
Testament parallels, the Lavabo at Mass is not
done out of obedience to the Old Law — "and
thus it is not observed in the same way [now] as
then."[88] Therefore, unlike in the Jewish sacrifices, the priest does not have his feet washed at
Mass, but only his hands.[89] This is both because
the hands can be washed more readily than the
feet, and also because, as Aristotle teaches in the

---

86 "Quia, ut Dionysius dicit, III cap. Eccles. Hier.,
extremitatum ablutio significat emundationem etiam a
minimis peccatis, secundum illud Ioan. XIII, *qui lotus est,
non indiget nisi ut pedes lavet*. Et talis emundatio requiritur ab
eo qui accedit ad hoc sacramentum." *ST* IIIa, Q. 83, a. 5, ad 1.

87 "Quod etiam significatur per confessionem quae
fit ante introitum Missae." *ST* IIIa, Q. 83, a. 5, ad 1. It
is also possible that St. Thomas has in mind not the
Lavabo at the Offertory, but rather the priest's washing
his hands before the Mass begins, which would underscore
the connection to the Confiteor. But his identifying this
washing as taking place "among the solemnities of the
Mass" ("inter Missarum solemnia") might militate against
that possibility. *ST* IIIa, Q. 83, a. 5, obj. 1. So might his
treating it together with the incensations. See *ST* IIIa, Q.
83, a. 5, obj. 2 & ad 2.

88 "Et ideo non eodem modo observatur sicut tunc."
ST IIIa, Q. 83, a. 5, ad 1.

89 "Praetermittitur enim pedum ablutio, et servatur
ablutio manuum." *ST* IIIa, Q. 83, a. 5, ad 1.

De Anima, "the hand is the organ of organs," and thus "all works are attributed to the hands."[90] St. Thomas then quotes from Psalm 25:6, which opens with the word *"Lavabo"*: *I shall wash my hands among the innocent.*[91]

Consummation (Preface–Reception)

With the Offertory or Oblation completed, at last the Mass begins to turn itself toward the consecration.[92] This turn begins, as we might expect by now, with a certain preparation. "Yet the preparation of the people and ministers and priest for so great a sacrament," St. Thomas says, "is done through the devout praise of God."[93] This preparation through devout praise consists of three things: the Preface dialogue, the Preface itself, and the Sanctus.[94]

The Preface dialogue begins with a *Dominus vobiscum*, which, St. Thomas says, must be

---

90 "Cum enim manus sit organum organorum, ut dicitur in III de anima, omnia opera attribuuntur manibus." *ST* IIIa, Q. 83, a. 5, ad 1.

91 "Unde et in Psalmo dicitur, *lavabo inter innocentes manus meas.*" *ST* IIIa, Q. 83, a. 5, ad 1.

92 "Deinde, circa consecrationem, quae supernaturali virtute agitur, primo excitatur populus ad devotionem in praefatione." *ST* IIIa, Q. 83, a. 4, c.

93 "Praeparatio autem populi et ministrorum et sacerdotis ad tantum sacramentum fit per devotam Dei laudem." *In IV Sent.*, d. 8, ex.

94 "Praeparatio autem populi et ministrorum et sacerdotis ad tantum sacramentum fit per devotam Dei laudem; unde in praefatione, in qua fit dicta praeparatio, tria continentur." *In IV Sent.*, d. 8, ex.

referred to everything from this moment until all the way after the reception of holy Communion, covering this whole great stretch of the Mass as though it were a single prayer.[95] The line of the Preface dialogue with which St. Thomas is most concerned is *Sursum corda* — literally, "Hearts up." He describes this as "the arousal of the people to praise, when the priest . . . spurs them on to the raising of the mind."[96] Against the objection that this stirring up of devotion is unfitting, since none of the other sacraments has anything equivalent to the *Sursum corda*, St. Thomas answers that the Mass is special for two reasons. First, "greater devotion is required in this sacrament than in the other sacraments, on account of the fact that the whole Christ is contained in this sacrament," whereas the other sacraments contain shares in Christ's power but not Christ himself.[97] Second, "more common [devotion is required in this sacrament than in the other sacraments], because in this

---

95 "*Dominus vobiscum*, quod ad totam hanc tertiam partem referendum est." *In IV Sent.*, d. 8, ex.

96 "Primo populi excitatio ad laudem, ubi sacerdos . . . inducit ad mentis erectionem, dicens: *sursum corda.*" *In IV Sent.*, d. 8, ex. See also *ST* IIIa, Q. 83, a. 4, c: "Primo excitatur populus ad devotionem in praefatione, unde et monetur sursum corda habere ad dominum."

97 "In hoc sacramento maior devotio requiritur quam in aliis sacramentis, propter hoc quod in hoc sacramento totus Christus continetur." *ST* IIIa, Q. 83, a. 4, ad 5. On the comparison between the Mass and other sacraments, see also *ST* IIIa, Q. 65, a. 3.

sacrament there is required the devotion of the whole people, for whom the sacrifice is offered, and not only of those receiving the sacrament, as in the other sacraments."[98] To justify his position, St. Thomas also quotes from the patristic authority of St. Cyprian: "The priest, before the Preface, prepares the minds of the brethren, saying, *Sursum corda*, so that when the people respond, *Habemus ad Dominum*, they might be admonished to think of nothing other than God."[99] Finally, St. Thomas notes that the priest's last line in the Preface dialogue, namely *Gratias agamus Domino Deo nostro*, is meant to move the people to thanksgiving.[100]

If the Preface dialogue was an incitement to praise, the Preface itself is the prayer that God should receive this praise.[101] Here the priest reasons with God, explaining that this praise is due to him, and that he should accept it because it is *vere dignum* [truly worthy or right] "by reason of his dominion," which is why the priest

---

98 "Et etiam communior, quia in hoc sacramento requiritur devotio totius populi, pro quo sacrificium offertur, et non solum percipientium sacramentum, sicut in aliis sacramentis." *ST* IIIa, Q. 83, a. 4, ad 5.

99 "Et ideo, sicut Cyprianus dicit, *sacerdos, praefatione praemissa, parat fratrum mentes, dicendo, sursum corda, ut, dum respondet plebs, habemus ad dominum, admoneatur nihil aliud se cogitare quam Deum.*" *ST* IIIa, Q. 83, a. 4, ad 5.

100 "inducit . . . ad gratiarum actionem, dicens: *gratias agamus Domino Deo nostro.*" *In IV Sent.*, d. 8, ex.

101 "Secundo Deum implorat ad laudem suscipiendum." *In IV Sent.*, d. 8, ex.

then adds, *Domine sancte*.[102] It is also *iustum*
[just] "by reason of his paternity," whence the
priest adds, *Pater omnipotens*.[103] It is *aequum*
[fair] "by reason of his deity," and so the priest
adds, *aeterne Deus*.[104] And it is *salutare* [salvific]
"by reason of the redemption," whence he adds,
per Christum Dominum nostrum.[105] At this point,
sometimes the Preface also includes something
special, "some other matter of praise according to what befits the solemnity," St. Thomas
observes, giving the example of the Preface for
the Assumption.[106] Lastly, the Preface looks to
the angels as the "example of praise": *per quem
maiestatem tuam laudant angeli*.

Once the priest has thus spurred the people
to praise, and has thus begged God to accept
this praise, now it is time for the praise itself,
namely the Sanctus. In both *Scriptum* and
Summa, St. Thomas sees the two halves of the
Sanctus as a doxological proclamation of the
Hypostatic Union. First, "the people break forth

---

102 "ostendens laudis debitum, dicens: *vere dignum*,
ratione Dominii (unde subdit: *Domine sancte*)." *In IV Sent.*,
d. 8, ex.
103 "*justum* ratione paternitatis (unde subdit: *pater
omnipotens*)." *In IV Sent.*, d. 8, ex.
104 "*aequum*, ratione deitatis (unde subdit: *aeterne
Deus*)." *In IV Sent.*, d. 8, ex.
105 "*salutare*, ratione redemptionis (unde subdit: *per
Christum Dominum nostrum*)." *In IV Sent.*, d. 8, ex.
106 "Quandoque vero adjungitur aliqua alia laudis
materia secundum congruentiam solemnitatis, sicut: *et
te in assumptione Beatae Mariae semper Virginis collaudare*."
In IV Sent., d. 8, ex.

in the praises" of Christ according to his divine nature, "taking up the words of the angels" from Isaiah 6:3: *Sanctus, sanctus, sanctus Dominus Deus exercituum* — or in Hebrew, *Sabaoth*. [107] Second, the people praise Christ in his human nature, "taking up the words of the children in Matthew 21:10: *benedictus qui venit in nomine Domini*." [108] Thus, for St. Thomas, the Sanctus combines the words of seraphim with those of the *pueri Hebraeorum*, the highest and the lowest along the created intellectual hierarchy, to praise the Lord who has taken up our lowly humanity into his loftiest Godhead.

At long last, the Mass arrives at the Roman Canon, which St. Thomas believes is prayed in silence because this "expresses the counsel of the Jews plotting the death of Christ," or else that "of the disciples, who did not dare to confess Christ openly." [109] Before we proceed to these silent words of the Canon, however,

---

107 "Tertio populus laudes exsolvit divinitatis, assumens angelorum verba: *sanctus, sanctus, sanctus Dominus Deus exercituum*, Isa. 6, 3." *In IV Sent.*, d. 8, ex. See also *ST* IIIa, Q. 83, a. 4, c: "Et ideo, finita praefatione, populus cum devotione laudat divinitatem Christi cum Angelis, dicens, sanctus, sanctus, sanctus."

108 "et humanitatis Christi, assumens verba puerorum, Matth. 21, 10: *benedictus qui venit in nomine Domini*." *In IV Sent.*, d. 8, ex. See also *ST* IIIa, Q. 83, a. 4, c: "et humanitatem cum pueris, dicens, benedictus qui venit."

109 "Tacita etiam locutio exprimit consilium Judaeorum mortem Christi machinantium, vel discipulorum, qui palam Christum confiteri non audebant." *In IV Sent.*, d. 12, ex.

first it is necessary to consider the gestures pre-
scribed for the priest during this great eucharistic prayer. In particular, we must consider
the many crosses he makes over the species, of
which there are eight different sets. Nor is this
mere useless repetition, because, St. Thomas
says, "The priest in the celebration of the Mass
uses the sign of the cross to express the Passion of Christ, which was terminated upon the
cross. Yet the Passion of Christ was enacted
through certain, as it were, steps."[110] First of
all, the priest makes three signs of the cross
at the beginning of the Canon, at the words
*haec dona, haec munera, haec sancta sacrificia illi-
bata*. On St. Thomas's telling, this set is done
"to signify the triple handing over of Christ,
namely by God, by Judas, and by the Jews."[111]
Second, the priest makes three signs of the
cross over both species together, at the words
benedictam, adscriptam, ratam, and then just
after that, one sign of the cross each over each
of the two species, at the words *corpus* and

---

110 "Sacerdos in celebratione Missae utitur crucesignatione ad exprimendam passionem Christi, quae ad
crucem est terminata. Est autem passio Christi quibusdam
quasi gradibus peracta." *ST* IIIa, Q. 83, a. 5, ad 3.

111 "ad significandum trinam traditionem Christi,
scilicet a Deo, Juda, et Judaeis." *In IV Sent.*, d. 12, ex. See
also *ST* IIIa, Q. 83, a. 5, ad 3: "Nam primo fuit Christi
traditio, quae facta est a Deo, a Iuda, et a Iudaeis. Quod
significat trina crucesignatio super illa verba, *haec dona,
haec munera, haec sancta sacrificia illibata*." On this triple
handing over, see *ST* IIIa, Q. 47.

sanguis respectively. The three here, St. Thomas says, are "to show that Christ was sold to three, namely the priests, the scribes, and the Pharisees."[112] Alternatively, it could be "to show the price of the sale, namely thirty denarii."[113] Whereas the two that follow are "to show the seller and the one sold."[114] Third, there are two signs of the cross at the words *benedixit et fregit*, "one over the body, another over the blood, to show that this sacrament prevails for the health of body and of soul"[115]—or perhaps, to designate "the pre-signification of the Passion of Christ made at the supper."[116]

Those first three sets of signs of the cross occur before the consecration. The rest come

---

112 "ad ostendendum quod tribus Christus est venditus, scilicet sacerdotibus, Scribis, et Pharisaeis." *In IV Sent.*, d. 12, ex. See also *ST* IIIa, Q. 83, a. 5, ad 3: "Secundo fuit Christi venditio. Est autem venditus sacerdotibus, Scribis et Pharisaeis. Ad quod significandum fit iterum trina crucesignatio super illa verba, *benedictam, adscriptam, ratam.*"

113 "Vel ad ostendendum pretium venditionis, scilicet triginta denarios." *ST* IIIa, Q. 83, a. 5, ad 3.

114 "ad ostendendum venditorem et venditum." *In IV Sent.*, d. 12, ex. See also *ST* IIIa, Q. 83, a. 5, ad 3: "Additur autem et duplex super illa verba, *ut nobis corpus et sanguis*, etc., ad designandam personam Iudae venditoris et Christi venditi."

115 "unam super corpus, aliam super sanguinem, ad ostendendum quod hoc sacramentum valet ad salutem corporis et animae." *In IV Sent.*, d. 12, ex.

116 "Tertio autem fuit praesignatio passionis Christi facta in cena. Ad quod designandum, fiunt tertio duae cruces, una in consecratione corporis, alia in consecratione sanguinis, ubi utrobique dicitur benedixit." *ST* IIIa, Q. 83, a. 5, ad 3.

after, and so it is important for St. Thomas to
clarify that, when the priest signs the cross over
the confected sacrament, he "does not use the
sign of the cross to bless and consecrate, but
only to commemorate the power of the cross
and the mode of the Passion of Christ." [117] Thus
the first three sets represented various preparations for the Passion, whereas the remaining
signs of the cross represent the Passion itself. [118]
The fourth of the eight sets comes at the words
*hostiam puram, hostiam sanctam, hostiam immac-
ulatam, Panem sanctum vitae aeternae, et Calicem
salutis perpetuae*, at which the priest makes five
signs of the cross, which, St. Thomas says, are
"to represent the five wounds." [119] Fifth, there
are two signs of the cross at the words *sacrosanctum Filii tui corpus et sanguinem sumpserimus*,
"to signify the chains and scourgings of Christ"
respectively, after which the priest signs himself
once at the words *omni benedictione*, "because

---

117 "Sacerdos post consecrationem non utitur crucesignatione ad benedicendum et consecrandum, sed solum
ad commemorandum virtutem crucis et modum passionis
Christi, ut ex dictis patet." *ST* IIIa, Q. 83, a. 5, ad 4. See
also *In IV Sent.*, d. 13, ex: "Hostiae benedictio non est
principaliter a sacerdote, sed a Deo."

118 "Quarto autem fuit ipsa passio Christi." *ST* IIIa,
Q. 83, a. 5, ad 3.

119 "ad repraesentandum quinque plagas." *In IV Sent.*,
d. 12, ex. See also *ST* IIIa, Q. 83, a. 5, ad 3: "Unde, ad
repraesentandum quinque plagas, fit quarto quintuplex
crucesignatio super illa verba, *hostiam puram, hostiam sanctam, hostiam immaculatam, panem sanctum vitae aeternae, et
calicem salutis perpetuae*."

the wounds of Christ are our medicine."[120] However, St. Thomas also offers a couple of alternative readings of this set, taking the three together as signifying "the threefold prayer" that Christ prayed in Gethsemane,[121] or else as "the stretching of his body, and the pouring out of his blood, and the fruit of the Passion."[122] Sixth, the priest makes three signs of the cross at the words *sanctificas, vivificas, benedicis*. St. Thomas finds a double symbol here, with the three crosses representing both "that the Jews said, *Crucify him*, three times, crucifying Christ by a word," and also that this took place "at the third hour."[123] It could also signify "the threefold prayer that he made upon the cross, one for his persecutors, when he said, *Father, forgive them* (Luke 23:34); second for liberation from death, when he said, *My God, my God, why have you forsaken me?* (Matt 27:46); the third pertains to the obtaining of glory, when he said, *Father, into*

---

120 "ad signandum vincula et flagella Christi; . . . quia Christi vulnera, nostra sunt medicamenta." *In IV Sent.*, d. 12, ex.

121 "Vel per has tres cruces significatur triplex oratio, qua Christus orasse legitur Matth. 26, passione imminente." *In IV Sent.*, d. 12, ex.

122 "Quinto, repraesentatur extensio corporis, et effusio sanguinis, et fructus passionis, per trinam cruces-ignationem quae fit super illis verbis, *corpus et sanguinem sumpserimus, omni benedictione* et cetera." *ST* IIIa, Q. 83, a. 5, ad 3.

123 "ad repraesentandum, quod Judaei ter dixerunt: *crucifige*, verbo crucifigentes Christum, quod fuit tertia hora." *In IV Sent.*, d. 12, ex.

your hands I commend my spirit (Luke 23:46)."[124]
Seventh, there are three signs of the cross at
the words *Per ipsum, et in ipso, et cum ipso*, to
represent his crucifixion "by the soldiers at
the sixth hour after a span of three hours."[125]
St. Thomas gives another explanation for this
set of three crosses too: "to represent his three
tortures, namely of passion, of propassion, and
of compassion" — in other words, his suffering,
his suffering for others, and his suffering with
others.[126] Eighth and last, the priest makes
two signs of the cross outside the chalice, at
the words *est tibi Deo Patri omnipotenti in unitate
Spiritus Sancti omnis honor et gloria*. St. Thomas

---

124 "Sexto, repraesentatur triplex oratio quam fecit
in cruce, unam pro persecutoribus, cum dixit, *pater, ignosce
illis*; secundam pro liberatione a morte, cum dixit, *Deus,
Deus meus, ut quid dereliquisti me?* Tertia pertinet ad adep-
tionem gloriae, cum dixit, *pater, in manus tuas commendo
spiritum meum*. Et ad hoc significandum, fit trina crucesignatio super illa verba, *sanctificas, vivificas, benedicis*, et
cetera." *ST* IIIa, Q. 83, a. 5, ad 3.

125 "ad repraesentandum secundam crucifixionem,
qua a militibus hora sexta post trium horarum spatium
crucifixus est." *In IV Sent.*, d. 12, ex. This "second crucifixion" refers to the carrying out of the call for his crucifixion,
which call is the beginning of the process, i.e. the "first crucifixion" — a traditional means of resolving the apparent
discrepancy between Mark's saying that he was crucified
at the third hour while the others have it at the sixth hour.
See also *ST* IIIa, Q. 83, a. 5, ad 3: "Septimo, repraesentantur
tres horae quibus pependit in cruce, scilicet a sexta hora
usque ad nonam. Et ad hoc significandum, fit iterum trina
crucesignatio ad illa verba, *per ipsum, et cum ipso, et in ipso*."

126 "vel ad repraesentandum tres ejus cruciatus, scilicet passionis, propassionis, compassionis." *In IV Sent.*,
d. 12, ex.

explains that these two are either "to represent the separation of soul from body, which was done at the ninth hour," or else "on account of the blood and water, which flowed forth from the side of Christ."[127] Summarizing all eight of these sets, or encompassing them under a general principle, St. Thomas says, "The consecration of this sacrament, and the reception of the sacrifice, of its fruit, proceed from the power of the cross of Christ. And thus, every time that mention is made of any of these, the priest uses the sign of the cross."[128]

So much, then, for the signs of the cross in the Roman Canon. We proceed now to consider its words. The Canon is comprised of eleven paragraphs: the Te Igitur, the Memento of the Living, the Communicantes, the Hanc Igitur, the Quam Oblationem, the Qui Pridie, the Unde et Memores, the Supra Quae, the Supplices Te Rogamus, the Memento of the Dead, and the Nobis Quoque — followed by a final doxology. As discussed above regarding the *divisio*

---

127 "ad repraesentandum separationem animae a corpore, quae facta est hora nona; . . . vel propter sanguinem et aquam, quae de latere Christi profluxerunt." *In IV Sent.*, d. 12, ex. See also *ST* IIIa, Q. 83, a. 5, ad 3: "Octavo autem, repraesentatur separatio animae a corpore, per duas cruces subsequentes extra calicem factas."

128 "Potest autem brevius dici quod consecratio huius sacramenti, et acceptio sacrificii, et fructus eius, procedit ex virtute crucis Christi. Et ideo, ubicumque fit mentio de aliquo horum, sacerdos crucesignatione utitur." *ST* IIIa, Q. 83, a. 5, ad 3.

Missae, in the *Sentences* St. Thomas divides these paragraphs into three groups, according to the classical sacramental distinction of *sacramentum tantum*, *res et sacramentum*, and *res tantum* — that is, "sacrament only," "reality and sacrament," and "reality only." [129] St. Thomas associates the *sacramentum tantum* with "the blessing of the matter offered," which he extends from the Te Igitur through the Hanc Igitur. [130] For the *res et sacramentum*, which goes from the Quam Oblationem through the Unde et Memores, he has "the consecration of the body and blood of Christ." [131] Finally, St. Thomas categorizes everything from the Supra Quae through the end of the Canon as "the petition for the effect of the sacrament," which he identifies as the *res tantum*. [132] In the *Summa Theologiae*, he dispenses with this tripartite division, now only signaling a change at the Quam Oblationem, which he views as the pivot point away from

---

129 "Illa autem pars quae perfectionem sacramenti continet, in tres dividitur, secundum tria quae sunt de integritate hujus sacramenti: scilicet aliquid quod est sacramentum tantum; aliquid quod est res et sacramentum; aliquid quod est res tantum." *In IV Sent.*, d. 8, ex.

130 "In prima ergo parte continetur benedictio oblatae materiae, quae est tantum sacramentum." *In IV Sent.*, d. 8, ex.

131 "In secunda corporis et sanguinis Christi consecratio, quod est res et sacramentum, ibi: *quam oblationem.*" *In IV Sent.*, d. 8, ex.

132 "In tertia, effectus sacramenti postulatio quod est res tantum, ibi: *supra quae propitio ac sereno vultu respicere digneris.*" *In IV Sent.*, d. 8, ex.

preparation and to "the consecration itself." [133]

In the Te Igitur, St. Thomas says that the priest "asks for the blessing of the oblation, which is called a *donum* [gift] given to us by God, a *munus* [offering] offered to God by us, a *sacrificium* [sacrifice] sanctified by God for our salvation." [134] This is also the part of the Canon in which "the priest secretly commemorates . . . those for whom this sacrifice is offered, namely for the universal Church, and for those who are set in high places, according to 1 Timothy 2:2." [135]

These commemorations continue into the Memento of the Living, in which the priest "asks for salvation for those offering, or for those for whom it is offered." [136] According to St. Thomas, this latter group embraces all "those for whose benefit the host is offered, both as regards the general state of the Church, and as regards special persons." [137]

---

133 "Deinde accedit ad ipsam consecrationem." *ST* IIIa, Q. 83, a. 4, c.

134 "Primo petit oblationis benedictionem, quae dicitur *donum* a Deo nobis datum, *munus* Deo a nobis oblatum, *sacrificium* ad nostram salutem a Deo sanctificatum." *In IV Sent.*, d. 8, ex.

135 "Deinde sacerdos secreto commemorat, primo quidem, illos pro quibus hoc sacrificium offertur, scilicet pro universali Ecclesia, et pro his qui in sublimitate sunt constituti, I Tim. II." *ST* IIIa, Q. 83, a. 4, c.

136 "Secundo petit *offerentibus*, sive pro quibus offertur, salutem, ibi: *in primis quae tibi offerimus*, etc." *In IV Sent.*, d. 8, ex.

137 "Primo commemorat eos pro quorum utilitate offertur hostia tam quantum ad generalem statum ecclesiae, quam quantum ad personas speciales, ibi: *memento*." *In IV*

The Communicantes likewise involves commemorations — hence its name — but now not of those who will benefit from it, but rather of "those in whose reverence it is offered," namely "the saints, whose patronage [the priest] implores for those mentioned above." [138] St. Thomas points out how fitting it is that this list of saints, who are invoked at the offering of the Mass, includes "the Virgin who offered Christ in the temple, the apostles who handed on the rite of offering to us, and the martyrs who offered themselves to God." [139] However, Thomas notices, it does not include confessors. He suggests two reasons for this omission: either "because the ancient Church did not celebrate them," or else "because they did not suffer like Christ, of whose Passion this sacrament is the memorial." [140]

For St. Thomas, the Hanc Igitur serves as a kind of conclusion. It brings to an end "the

---

Sent., d. 8, ex. See also *ST* IIIa, Q. 83, a. 4, c: "et specialiter quosdam qui offerunt vel pro quibus offertur."

138 "Secundo commemorat eos in quorum offertur reverentia, ibi: *communicantes.*" *In IV Sent.*, d. 8, ex. "Commemorat sanctos, quorum patrocinia implorat pro praedictis, cum dicit, communicantes et memoriam venerantes, et cetera." *ST* IIIa, Q. 83, a. 4, c.

139 "Et ponitur Virgo quae Christum in templo obtulit, apostoli qui ritum offerendi nobis tradiderunt, et martyres qui seipsos Deo obtulerunt." *In IV Sent.*, d. 8, ex.

140 "Non autem confessores, quia de eis antiquitus non solemnizabat ecclesia, vel quia non sunt passi sicut Christus, cujus passionis memoriale est hoc sacramentum." *In IV Sent.*, d. 8, ex.

petition" of these first four paragraphs of the
Canon, namely "that the oblation might be
made salvific for those for whom it is offered." [141]

The Quam Oblation, on the other hand,
signals the beginning of what "pertains to the
consecration." [142] Here "the power of the one
consecrating is implored," by which, in this
instance, St. Thomas means God. [143] There is
a question about how to understand the five
adjectives that the priest asks God to deign
to make this oblation: *benedictam, adscriptam,
ratam, rationabilem, acceptabilemque*. St. Thomas
offers three possible explanations, which are
distinguished once again according to *sacramentum tantum, res et sacramentum*, and *res
tantum* —though St. Thomas only makes this
principle of division explicit in one of the three
cases. [144] He begins from the *res et sacramentum*:
"the thing contained in this sacrament, namely
Christ" — who, St. Thomas says, "is the *benedictam* [blessed] host, immune to every stain of sin;
adscriptam [reckoned], that is, prefigured by the

---

141 "Petitionem concludit, cum dicit, hanc igitur
oblationem etc. ut fiat oblatio pro quibus offertur salutaris." *ST* IIIa, Q. 83, a. 4, c. See also *In IV Sent.*, d. 8, ex:
"Tertio concluditur expresse quid per oblationem hostiae
impetrandum petatur, ibi: *hanc igitur oblationem*, etc."
142 "Haec pars ad consecrationem pertinet." *In IV
Sent.*, d. 8, ex.
143 "Primo imploratur consecrantis virtus." *In IV
Sent.*, d. 8, ex.
144 "Alio modo possunt referri ad ipsam hostiam,
quae est sacramentum tantum." *In IV Sent.*, d. 8, ex.

figures of the Old Testament, and preordained
by divine predestination; *ratam* [fixed], because
not transitory; *rationabilem* [reasonable], on
account of its fittingness for placating; *acceptabilem* [acceptable], on account of its efficacy."[145]
Second, St. Thomas considers what these five
adjectives could mean if they were referred "to
the host itself, which is the *sacramentum tantum*" — which, St. Thomas says, the priest "asks
to be made *benedictam*, so that God would consecrate it; but to confirm it as regards memory: *adscriptam*; immovable as regards purpose:
ratam; so that he might accept it: *rationabilem*,
as regards the judgment of reason; *acceptabilem*,
as regards the pleasure of the will."[146] Lastly,
St. Thomas refers these terms to the *res tantum*,
"the effect" of the sacrament — whence the priest
says "*benedictam*, through which we are blessed;
adscriptam, through which we may be enrolled

---

145 "Verba autem illa quae ibi dicuntur: *benedictam,
adscriptam, ratam, rationabilem, acceptabilemque*, possunt
referri uno modo ad hoc quod est res contenta in hoc
sacramento, scilicet Christum, qui est hostia benedicta
ab omni macula peccati immunis; adscripta, idest praefigurata figuris veteris testamenti, et praedestinatione divina praeordinata; rata, quia non transitoria; rationabilis,
propter congruitatem ad placandum; acceptabilis, propter
efficaciam." *In IV Sent.*, d. 8, ex.

146 "Alio modo possunt referri ad ipsam hostiam,
quae est sacramentum tantum; quam petit fieri *benedictam*,
ut Deus eam consecret; sed ut confirmet quantum ad
memoriam: *adscriptam*; quantum ad propositum immobile: *ratam*; ut eam accepted: *rationabilem*, quantum ad
judicium rationis; *acceptabilem*, quantum ad beneplacitum
voluntatis." *In IV Sent.*, d. 8, ex.

in heaven; *ratam*, through which we may be counted among Christ's members; *rationabilem*, through which we may be saved from bestial sense; *acceptabilem*, through which we may be welcome before God."[147]

St. Thomas must also respond to an objection about the Quam Oblationem, namely that it is entirely unnecessary. Because the divine power operates in this sacrament infallibly, the objector says, there is no reason for the priest to ask for it to work.[148] St. Thomas's answer is twofold. First of all, he explains that it would be perfectly fine to ask for the divine power to work for the consecration, both because "the efficacy of the sacramental words can be impeded through the intention of the priest," and because, "regardless, it is not unfitting that we should ask of God what we know is most certainly going to be done, just like Christ, in John 17:1–5, asked for his glorification."[149] But

---

147 "Tertio modo possunt referri ad effectum; unde dicit, *benedictam*, per quam benedicimur; *adscriptam*, per quam in caelis ascribamur; *ratam*, per quam in membris Christi censeamur; *rationabilem*, per quam a bestiali sensu eruamur; *acceptabilem*, per quam Deo accepti simus." *In IV Sent.*, d. 8, ex. See also *ST* IIIa, Q. 83, a. 4, c: "In qua primo petit consecrationis effectum, cum dicit, quam oblationem tu Deus."

148 See *ST* IIIa, Q. 83, a. 4, obj. 7.

149 "Efficacia verborum sacramentalium impediri potest per intentionem sacerdotis. Nec tamen est inconveniens quod a Deo petamus id quod certissime scimus ipsum facturum, sicut Christus, Ioan. XVII, petiit suam clarificationem." *ST* IIIa, Q. 83, a. 4, ad 7.

secondly, St. Thomas clarifies that this doesn't really matter in the case of the Quam Oblationem anyway, since the priest is not asking for the divine power to work in consecrating the holy Eucharist, but rather for the holy Eucharist to work in having its effect in the faithful. "The priest does not seem to be praying there that the consecration may be fulfilled," St. Thomas says, "but rather that it may be fruitful for us."[150] As evidence of this, he underscores the "*nobis*" in the line *ut nobis corpus et sanguis fiat*.[151] He then returns to the third way above of understanding the Quam Oblationem's five adjectives, that is, in terms of the benefits for the recipients.[152]

Finally, we arrive at the Qui Pridie, the paragraph of the Roman Canon that contains the words of institution, the most important part of holy Mass. It is perhaps surprising, therefore, that in both of St. Thomas Aquinas's *expositiones*

---

150 "Non tamen ibi videtur sacerdos orare ut consecratio impleatur, sed ut nobis fiat fructuosa." *ST* IIIa, Q. 83, a. 4, ad 7.

151 "unde signanter dicit, ut nobis corpus et sanguis fiat." *ST* IIIa, Q. 83, a. 4, ad 7.

152 "Et hoc significant verba quae praemittit dicens, hanc oblationem facere digneris benedictam, secundum Augustinum, idest, per quam benedicimur, scilicet per gratiam; adscriptam, idest, per quam in caelo adscribimur; ratam, idest, per quam visceribus Christi censeamur; rationabilem, idest, per quam a bestiali sensu exuamur; acceptabilem, idest, ut, qui nobis ipsis displicemus, per hanc acceptabiles eius unico filio simus." *ST* IIIa, Q. 83, a. 4, ad 7.

Missae, he passes over this section with a single sentence. In the *Scriptum,* we read, "The consecration is completed, at *Qui pridie quam pateretur, accepit panem.*"[153] In the *Summa*: "He performs the consecration through the words of the Savior, when he says, *Qui pridie* etc."[154] In fact, it seems the only reason St. Thomas says even this much is for the sake of his outline of the text, so that this paragraph of the Canon is accounted for. Why would St. Thomas effectively skip over this, the centerpiece of the entire Mass? There are, I believe, two reasons. First, his *expositiones Missae* are explicitly a consideration of *"ea quae circa hoc sacramentum dicuntur"* — "the things that are said *around* this sacrament."[155] They are treatments of the liturgical complement of the sacrament itself, the solemnities that surround the consecration. The words of institution, on the other hand, are not part of these surroundings, but part of the thing surrounded. They are the very form of the sacrament. Which comes to the second reason that St. Thomas does not treat the words of institution in his *expositiones Missae*: He has already treated them. Both in the *Sentences* commentary and in the *Summa Theologiae,*

---

153 "Secundo perficitur consecratio, ibi: *qui pridie quam pateretur, accepit panem.*" *In IV Sent.,* d. 8, ex.

154 "Secundo, consecrationem peragit per verba salvatoris, cum dicit, qui pridie, et cetera." *ST* IIIa, Q. 83, a. 4, c.

155 *ST* IIIa, Q. 83, a. 4, obj. 1 (emphasis added).

St. Thomas has made an extensive study of the
form of the sacrament before he comes to his
study of the eucharistic liturgy. In the *Sentences*,
this is in Book 4, Distinction 8, Question 2;
in the *Summa*, it is in *Tertia Pars*, Question 78.
Thus there is no need for St. Thomas to repeat
himself here, nor to consider what pertains to
the very being of the holy Eucharist, in this his
treatment of its liturgical well-being.[156]

Nevertheless, this moment of the consecration does provide an occasion to consider a few
other relevant matters. Among these is a gesture
that the priest begins now, and maintains until
after the distribution of holy Communion: the
joining of his canonical digits. Like with many
actions of the Mass, St. Thomas teaches that
this "pertains to reverence for the sacrament."[157]
The priest "joins his digits after the consecration," St. Thomas says, "namely his thumb and
index finger, with which he had touched the
consecrated body of Christ."[158] He holds these
fingers together all the way until the ablutions
"so that, if any particle should have stuck to his
fingers, it would not be lost."[159]

See again *ST* IIIa, Q. 66, a. 10, ad 4.

157 "Quod pertinet ad reverentiam sacramenti." *ST*
IIIa, Q. 83, a. 5, ad 5.

158 "Digitos autem iungit post consecrationem, scilicet pollicem cum indice, quibus corpus Christi consecratum
tetigerat." *ST* IIIa, Q. 83, a. 5, ad 5.

159 "ut, si qua particula digitis adhaeserat, non dispergatur." *ST* IIIa, Q. 83, a. 5, ad 5.

St. Thomas also answers a few objections concerning the consecration. One is about its placement within the Roman Canon, namely why it is in the middle rather than at the end, the latter of which would seem to be the more honorable place, so that the whole Canon might build up to it.[160] St. Thomas answers, with recourse to Pope Innocent III, that "the words of consecration . . . are placed in the middle to observe the order of history."[161] To make sense of this solution, one needs to recall what St. Thomas had said about the various signs of the cross that the priest makes during the Canon: The first three sets, which come before the consecration, pertain to the preparation for Christ's Passion, whereas the five sets that follow the consecration pertain to the Passion itself. And because "the words of the Canon pertain principally to consecrating the Eucharist, but the signs to recalling the history," it is fitting that the words of institution should be placed here, in between the preparations for the Passion and the Passion itself, since that is in fact the moment during Holy Week in which this sacrament was instituted, the evening of Holy Thursday: *Qui pridie quam pateretur.*[162]

---

160 "quae in fine ponenda essent quasi complementum totius." *In IV Sent.*, d. 12, ex.

161 "Verba consecrationis . . . in medio ponuntur ad historiae ordinem observandum." *In IV Sent.*, d. 12, ex.

162 "Verba canonis ad Eucharistiam consecrandam principaliter pertinent, sed signa ad historiam recolendam." *In IV Sent.*, d. 12, ex.

Therefore, as Pope Innocent says in the text that St. Thomas references, the consecration is found in the middle *"quasi cor canonis"* — "like the heart of the Canon."[163]

Another objection about the words of consecration is that they are totally sufficient on their own, since they are the words of Christ himself, and thus they do not need any of this liturgical window dressing.[164] In other words, the Mass should be just the consecration itself, with nothing before or after. We have already seen St. Thomas explain that all the sacramental rites pertain to the well-being of the sacraments, over and above their mere being, since these precious gifts deserve more than the bare minimum.[165] But in the case of the Mass, he also teaches that the rest of the liturgical rite has a purpose for the recipients. Granted the words of institution are Christ's own words, we still need more than just these, not in order to confect the holy Eucharist, but in order "to contribute to the preparation of the people receiving."[166] It is precisely because Christ's

---

163 Innocent III, *De sacro altaris mysterio*, Bk. 5, ch. 2 (PL 217, col. 888).

164 "Inconvenienter ordinentur ea quae circa hoc sacramentum dicuntur. Hoc enim sacramentum verbis Christi consecratur, ut Ambrosius dicit, in libro de sacramentis. Non ergo debent aliqua alia in hoc sacramento dici quam verba Christi." *ST* IIIa, Q. 83, a. 4, obj. 1.

165 See again *ST* IIIa, Q. 66, a. 10, ad 4.

166 "Consecratio solis verbis Christi conficitur. Alia

words are sufficient to cause so great a sacrament, that other words are needed to make us ready to receive it.

A further objector complains that the *Qui pridie* should neither add to nor deviate from what we know about Christ's institution of this sacrament from the scriptures.[167] For example, the objection claims, there should be no mention of Christ raising his eyes, since the Last Supper accounts do not say this.[168] Nor should the word *manducate* [eat] be substituted for the Gospels' *comedite* [eat], and for the same reason the vocative *omnes* [all of you] should not be added to Christ's scriptural command to take and eat.[169] St. Thomas resolves this issue by referencing John 21:15, which, in Thomas's paraphrase, teaches that "many things were done or said by the Lord that the Evangelists did not write down."[170] This includes the detail

---

vero necesse fuit addere ad praeparationem populi sumentis, ut dictum est." *ST* IIIa, Q. 83, a. 4, ad 1.

167 "Verba et facta Christi nobis per Evangelium innotescunt. Sed quaedam dicuntur circa consecrationem huius sacramenti quae in Evangeliis non ponuntur . . . . Inconvenienter ergo huiusmodi verba dicuntur in celebratione huius sacramenti." *ST* IIIa, Q. 83, a. 4, obj. 2.

168 "Non enim legitur in Evangelio quod Christus in institutione huius sacramenti oculos ad caelum levaverit." *ST* IIIa, Q. 83, a. 4, obj. 2.

169 "Similiter etiam in Evangeliis dicitur, accipite et comedite, nec ponitur omnes, cum in celebratione huius sacramenti dicatur, elevatis oculis in caelum, et iterum, accipite et manducate ex hoc omnes." *ST* IIIa, Q. 83, a. 4, obj. 2.

170 "Sicut dicitur Ioan. ult., multa sunt a domino

about Christ's lifting his eyes to heaven, which, St. Thomas says, "nevertheless the Church has from the tradition of the apostles."[171] St. Thomas defends this by comparing it to other stories from the Gospels: "For it seems reasonable that he who raised his eyes to the Father at the raising of Lazarus, in John 11:41, and in the prayer that he made for his disciples, in John 17:1, much more would do so at the institution of this sacrament, since this is more powerful."[172] As regards the *manducate*-for-*comedite* swap, St. Thomas says that this is no problem because they are synonyms anyway, and besides this line is not even part of the form.[173] The addition of the word *omnes* is also unobjectionable, because it "is understood in the words of the Gospel, although granted it is not expressed."[174] St. Thomas simply plays out the

facta vel dicta quae Evangelistae non scripserunt." *ST* IIIa, Q. 83, a. 4, ad 2.

171 "Inter quae fuit hoc quod dominus oculos levavit in caelum in cena, quod tamen Ecclesia ex traditione apostolorum habuit." *ST* IIIa, Q. 83, a. 4, ad 2.

172 "Rationabile enim videtur ut qui in suscitatione Lazari, ut habetur Ioan. XI, et in oratione quam pro discipulis fecit, Ioan. XVII, oculos levavit ad patrem, in huius sacramenti institutione multo magis hoc fecerit, tanquam in re potiori." *ST* IIIa, Q. 83, a. 4, ad 2.

173 "Quod autem dicitur manducate, et non comedite, non differt quantum ad sensum. Nec multum refert quid dicatur, praesertim cum verba illa non sint de forma." *ST* IIIa, Q. 83, a. 4, ad 2. On this line's not being included in the form of the sacrament, see *ST* IIIa, Q. 78, a. 4, ad 2 & ad 4.

174 "Quod autem additur omnes, intelligitur in verbis Evangelii, licet non exprimatur." *ST* IIIa, Q. 83, a. 4, ad 2.

reasoning from John 6:54: *Unless you should eat the flesh of the Son of Man, you shall not have life in you.* [175] The implication is that all, *omnes*, are indeed supposed to take and eat, since anyone who does not do so is spiritually dead.

The first paragraph of the Roman Canon after the consecration is the Unde et Memores. In the *Sentences*, St. Thomas describes this as the part of the Canon in which "the commemoration of the thing consecrated is expounded." [176] In the *Summa Theologiae*, he sees this as the place where the priest "excuses himself of presumption through obedience to the mandate of Christ." [177] St. Thomas also takes note of the distinctive posture of the priest during the Unde et Memores: He is cruciform. As St. Thomas explains, "Because the Lord commanded that this sacrament be carried out in memory of his death, thus immediately after the consecration, [the priest] represents the effigy of the cross by the extension of his arms." [178]

---

175 "quia ipse dixerat, Ioan. VI, *nisi manducaveritis carnem filii hominis, non habebitis vitam in vobis.*" *ST* IIIa, Q. 83, a. 4, ad 2.

176 "Tertio exponitur rei consecratae commemoratio, ibi: *unde et memores*, etc." *In IV Sent.*, d. 8, ex.

177 "Tertio, excusat praesumptionem per obedientiam ad mandatum Christi, cum dicit, unde et memores." *ST* IIIa, Q. 83, a. 4, c.

178 "Et quia Dominus hoc sacramentum in mortis suae memoriam exercendum mandavit, ideo statim post consecrationem brachiorum extensione crucis effigiem repraesentat." *In IV Sent.*, d. 12, ex. See also *ST* IIIa, Q. 83,

Next is the Supra Quae, in which the celebrant "asks that this sacrifice, having been completed, may be acceptable to God." [179] There is also an objection leveled against one line of the Supra Quae, in which the priest asks God to accept this sacrifice as he accepted those of Abel, Abraham, and Melchisedech. But the New Law sacrifice is better than the Old, the objector remarks, and so it is inappropriate to drag it down to the level of these Old Testament figures. [180] St. Thomas certainly agrees that, "of itself, this sacrifice is to be preferred to all the ancient sacrifices." [181] "Nevertheless," he says, "the sacrifices of the ancients were most acceptable to God from their devotion. The priest asks, therefore, that this sacrifice might be acceptable to God from the devotion of those offering, just as those others were acceptable to God." [182] Thus the petition in reference to Abel,

---

a. 5, ad 5: " Quod enim sacerdos brachia extendit post consecrationem, significat extensionem brachiorum Christi in cruce."

179 "Quarto, petit hoc sacrificium peractum esse Deo acceptum, cum dicit, supra quae propitio, et cetera." *ST* IIIa, Q. 83, a. 4, c. See also *In IV Sent.*, d. 8, ex: "Primo petit acceptari sacramentum, quod est gratiae causa."

180 "Sacrificium novae legis multo est excellentius quam sacrificium antiquorum patrum. Inconvenienter ergo sacerdos petit quod hoc sacrificium habeatur sicut sacrificium Abel, Abrahae et Melchisedech." *ST* IIIa, Q. 83, a. 4, obj. 8.

181 "Hoc sacrificium ex seipso praeferatur omnibus antiquis sacrificiis." *ST* IIIa, Q. 83, a. 4, ad 8.

182 "Tamen sacrificia antiquorum fuerunt Deo acceptissima ex eorum devotione. Petit ergo sacerdos ut hoc

Abraham, and Melchisedech should be taken as a prayer for those fruits that come *ex opere operantis*, although granted in itself this sacrament works *ex opere operato*.

The following paragraph of the Canon is the Supplices Te Rogamus. The *Scriptum* describes the Supplices as the request "that the gift of grace be given."[183] The *Summa* description is narrower, calling it a request "for the effect of this sacrifice and sacrament . . . as regards those receiving."[184] In terms of bodily posture, here the priest "joins his hands together and bows down, praying submissively and humbly," which St. Thomas believes "designates the humility and obedience of Christ, out of which he suffered."[185] What most interests St. Thomas in the Supplices, however, is the command to God that he command his holy angel to take these gifts to the heavenly altar: *Iube ergo haec perferri per manus sancti angeli tui in sublime altare tuum*. First of all, St. Thomas has to defend this against the charge that it would mean moving either the eucharistic species or

---

sacrificium acceptetur Deo ex devotione offerentium, sicut illa accepta fuerunt Deo." *ST* IIIa, Q. 83, a. 4, ad 8.

183 "Petit dari gratiae donum, ibi: *supplices te rogamus*." *In IV Sent.*, d. 8, ex.

184 "Quinto, petit huius sacrificii et sacramenti effectum, primo quidem, quantum ad ipsos sumentes, cum dicit, supplices te rogamus." *ST* IIIa, Q. 83, a. 4, c.

185 "Quod autem manus interdum iungit, et inclinat se, suppliciter et humiliter orans, designat humilitatem et obedientiam Christi, ex qua passus est." *ST* IIIa, Q. 83, a. 5, ad 5.

Christ's true body to heaven. [186] That defense is
easily made, since in the case of the species, they
are not taken away, and in the case of Christ's
true body, it never left heaven in the first place. [187]
Rather, St. Thomas says, the priest "asks this for
the mystical body, namely that which is signified
in this sacrament," the Church. [188] In terms of
the *per manus sancti angeli tui*, St. Thomas sees
two possibilities for what this angelic reference
could mean: On the one hand, it could refer
to the ministry of the angels at holy Mass; on
the other, it could indicate Christ himself. If it
is about the angels, then of course there is no
suggestion of an angel consecrating the holy
Eucharist, "because it does not have this kind
of power," but rather it is about the angels pre-
senting "the prayers of the priest and the people
to God, according to Revelation 8:4: *There arose
fragrant smoke in the sight of the Lord from the
hand of an angel, which are the prayers of the holy
ones.*" [189] If this is correct, then *in sublime altare*

---

186 "Corpus Christi, sicut non incoepit esse in hoc
sacramento per loci mutationem, ut supra dictum est,
ita etiam nec esse desinit. Inconvenienter ergo sacerdos
petit, *iube haec perferri per manus sancti Angeli tui in sublime
altare tuum.*" *ST* IIIa, Q. 83, a. 4, obj. 9.

187 "Sacerdos non petit quod species sacramentales
deferantur in caelum; neque corpus Christi verum, quod
ibi esse non desinit." *ST* IIIa, Q. 83, a. 4, ad 9.

188 "Sed petit hoc pro corpore mystico, quod scilicet
in hoc sacramento significatur." *ST* IIIa, Q. 83, a. 4, ad 9.

189 "Angelus sacris mysteriis interesse credendus est,
non ut consecret, quia hujusmodi potestatem non habet,

tuum could also mean two things: The priest is
asking that the mystical body be moved either
"to the Church triumphant, into which we are
asking to be transferred, or else to God himself,
since we are asking to participate in him." [190]
In both *Scriptum* and *Summa*, St. Thomas connects the latter possibility with Exodus 20:26,
in which "God himself is called the altar on
high": *not ascending to my altar by grades* — "that
is," St. Thomas says, "you shall not make grades
in the Trinity." [191] Finally, St. Thomas considers
the possibility that the holy angel here is not
literally an angel at all, but that this is a figure for
Christ — "who," Thomas declares, "is the Angel

---

sed ut orationes sacerdotis et populi Deo repraesentet,
secundum illud Apoc. 8, 4: *ascendit fumus aromatum in
conspectu Domini de manu angeli, quae sunt orationes sanctorum.*" *In IV Sent.*, d. 13, ex. See also *ST* IIIa, Q. 83, a. 4,
ad 9: "ut scilicet orationes et populi et sacerdotis Angelus
assistens divinis mysteriis Deo repraesentet; secundum
illud Apoc. VIII, *ascendit fumus incensorum de oblationibus
sanctorum de manu Angeli.*"

190 "Sublime autem altare Dei dicitur vel ipsa Ecclesia
triumphans, in quam transferri petimus, vel ipse Deus,
cuius participationem petimus." *ST* IIIa, Q. 83, a. 4, ad 9.
See also *In IV Sent.*, d. 13, ex: "Petit ergo sacerdos ut *haec*,
idest significata per haec, scilicet corpus mysticum, *per
manus angeli*, idest ministerio angelorum, perferantur *in
altare sublime*, idest in ecclesiam triumphantem, vel in
participationem divinitatis plenam."

191 "quia Deus ipse altare sublime dicitur; Exod. 20,
26: *non ascendes ad altare meum per gradus*; idest, in Trinitate non facies gradus." *In IV Sent.*, d. 13, ex. See also *ST*
IIIa, Q. 83, a. 4, ad 9: "de hoc enim altari dicitur Exod.
XX, *non ascendes ad altare meum per gradus*, idest, in Trinitate gradus non facies."

of great counsel in Isaiah 9:6 in the Septuagint, who joins his mystical body to God the Father, and to the Church triumphant." [192]

The next paragraph is the Memento of the Dead. Here, St. Thomas says, the priest "asks for the effect of glory . . . for those already dead." [193] He notes that it is important to pray for them, in particular, because they "can no longer receive" this sacrament themselves. [194]

The final paragraph of the Canon is the Nobis Quoque. In the *Sentences*, St. Thomas has this as the petition for "the effect of glory . . . for those still living." [195] Once again, however, the *Summa Theologiae* is much narrower, applying it "specifically to those priests offering" Masses. [196]

---

192 "Vel per angelum ipse Christus intelligitur, qui est magni consilii angelus, Isai. 9, 6, juxta 70, qui corpus suum mysticum Deo patri conjungit, et ecclesiae triumphanti." *In IV Sent.*, d. 13, ex. See also *ST* IIIa, Q. 83, a. 4, ad 9: "Vel per Angelum intelligitur ipse Christus, qui est magni consilii Angelus, qui corpus suum mysticum Deo patri coniungit et Ecclesiae triumphanti."

193 "Effectum autem gloriae primo petit jam mortuis, ibi, *memento*." *In IV Sent.*, d. 8, ex.

194 "secundo, quantum ad mortuos, qui iam sumere non possunt, cum dicit, memento etiam, domine, etc." *ST* IIIa, Q. 83, a. 4, c.

195 "Effectum autem gloriae . . . petit . . . adhuc vivis, ibi: *nobis quoque peccatoribus*." *In IV Sent.*, d. 8, ex.

196 "tertio, specialiter quantum ad ipsos sacerdotes offerentes, cum dicit, nobis quoque peccatoribus et cetera." *ST* IIIa, Q. 83, a. 4, c. Despite the plural, it is unlikely that St. Thomas is conceiving of multiple priests concelebrating a single Mass, and more likely that he is simply speaking in terms of all Masses considered together. For St. Thomas on concelebration, see *ST* IIIa, Q. 82, a. 2.

The Roman Canon closes with a final doxology. "The Canon of the Mass is completed," St. Thomas says, "after the custom of other prayers, in Christ."[197] Thus does this doxology begin with the words *Per Christum Dominum nostrum*. Such a Christological invocation is supremely fitting, according to St. Thomas, because it is through Christ that "this sacrament has its origin."[198] This is true both with regard to the sacrament's "substance—whence the priest says *creas* [you create] on account of the being of nature, *sanctificas* [you sanctify] on account of the being of the sacrament"; as well as with regard to the sacrament's "power—whence he says *vivificas* [you enliven] on account of the effect of grace, which is the life of the soul; *benedicis* [you bless] on account of the increase of grace; and as regards operation or use, whence he says *et praestas nobis* [you grant to us]."[199] Thus concludes St. Thomas's treatment of the Roman Canon.

With the Canon completed, the Mass moves on to the rites for the reception of holy Communion.

---

197 "Completur autem canon Missae more aliarum orationum in Christo, ibi: *per Christum Dominum nostrum.*" *In IV Sent.*, d. 8, ex.

198 "per quem hoc sacramentum originem habet." *In IV Sent.*, d. 8, ex.

199 "et quantum ad substantiam; unde dicit, *creas* propter esse naturae; *sanctificas*, propter esse sacramenti: et quantum ad virtutem; unde dicit, *vivificas*, propter effectum gratiae, quae est vita animae; *benedicis*, propter gratiae augmentum; et quantum ad operationem, sive usum; unde dicit: *et praestas nobis.*" *In IV Sent.*, d. 8, ex.

Probably unsurprisingly by now, the majority of these rites pertain to the preparation for this reception.[200] St. Thomas distinguishes the preparation of the people to receive the sacrament into two parts: a preparation through prayer and a preparation through peace.[201] This prayer consists of the Lord's Prayer and the priest's *Libera nos*; the peace consists of the Pax and the Agnus Dei.

As regards the Lord's Prayer, St. Thomas names this "the common prayer of the whole people."[202] He focuses especially on the line *Panem nostrum quotidianum da nobis hodie*: In the Lord's Prayer, he says, "we ask that our daily bread should be given to us."[203] Complementing this, the priest himself then prays the *Libera*

---

200 "Hic ponitur sacramenti perceptio, ad quam praemittitur praeparatio communis et specialis." *In IV Sent.*, d. 8, ex. "Deinde agitur de perceptione sacramenti. Et primo quidem, praeparatur populus ad percipiendum." *ST* IIIa, Q. 83, a. 4, c.

201 "Primo quidem, per orationem . . . . Secundo, praeparatur populus per pacem." *ST* IIIa, Q. 83, a. 4, c. In the *Sentences*, St. Thomas actually calls this a threefold division, but it amounts to the same thing, since all he does is number separately the Lord's Prayer and the priest's *Libera nos*, both of which he puts under the general heading of prayer in the *Summa*. See *In IV Sent.*, d. 8, ex: "Communis triplex."

202 "Primo quidem, per orationem communem totius populi, quae est oratio dominica." *ST* IIIa, Q. 83, a. 4, c.

203 "in qua petimus panem nostrum quotidianum nobis dari." *ST* IIIa, Q. 83, a. 4, c. See also *In IV Sent.*, d. 8, ex: "Primo enim ponitur sacramenti petitio in oratione Dominica, in qua dicitur: *panem nostrum quotidianum da nobis hodie*."

nos "for the people," in which he asks for "the expiation of those receiving."[204]

The preparation through peace begins with the priest's *Pax Domini sit semper vobiscum*, and it is completed by the choir's chanting of the Agnus Dei, which of course terminates in the petition *Dona nobis pacem*.[205] It is appropriate that peace should precede the receiving of the holy Eucharist, St. Thomas observes, "for this is the sacrament of unity and peace."[206] It is also fitting that it should be begun by the priest but finished by the choir, "because the peace of Christ surpasses every sense," and so no single speaker suffices to express it on his own.[207] St. Thomas sees this Pax as the fulfillment of a certain symbolic triptych, depicting the three theological virtues in different parts of the Mass, where the Gloria pertains to hope, the Credo to faith, and the Pax to charity.[208]

---

204 "Secundo percipientium expiatio per orationem sacerdotis: *libera nos*." *In IV Sent.*, d. 8, ex. "Et etiam privatam, quam specialiter sacerdos pro populo offert, cum dicit, libera nos, quaesumus, domine." *ST* IIIa, Q. 83, a. 4, c.

205 "tertio pacis adimpletio, ibi: *pax Domini* . . . . Ideo pacis petitio a sacerdote inchoatur, cum dicit *pax Domini*, et a choro completur, cum dicitur, *agnus Dei*." *In IV Sent.*, d. 8, ex. See also *ST* IIIa, Q. 83, a. 4, c: "Secundo, praeparatur populus per pacem, quae datur dicendo, agnus Dei."

206 "Est enim hoc sacramentum unitatis et pacis." *ST* IIIa, Q. 83, a. 4, c.

207 "Quia pax Christi exsuperat omnem sensum, ideo pacis petitio a sacerdote inchoatur . . . et a choro completur." *In IV Sent.*, d. 8, ex.

208 "Et sic tria a sacerdote incepta prosequitur, scilicet, *gloria in excelsis*, quod pertinet ad spem; *credo in unum*

However, St. Thomas notes, "in Masses for the dead . . . the Pax is omitted," since in such requiems "this sacrifice is offered not for present peace, but for the rest of the dead."[209] In terms of the threefold Agnus Dei, St. Thomas says that the first two lines are pleading for God's mercy against the double "misery of fault and of sin," and the third line is begging for "peace as regards the accomplishment of all good."[210]

Before, during, and after the priest's intoning of *Pax Domini sit semper vobiscum*, he is also occupied with an important set of actions, known collectively as the Fraction Rite, in which he breaks the host in three and puts the smallest of those into the chalice. One objector worries that this is inappropriate, since it seems to introduce division into the body of Christ.[211] But St. Thomas explains that the breaking of the host does no such thing, instead signifying three beautiful realities: "first of all, the very division of the body of Christ, which was made in the Passion; second, the distinction of the mystical body according to various states; and

---

Deum, quod pertinet ad fidem; *pax Domini*, quod pertinet ad caritatem." *In IV Sent.*, d. 8, ex.

209 "In Missis autem defunctorum, in quibus hoc sacrificium offertur non pro pace praesenti, sed pro requie mortuorum, pax intermittitur." *ST* IIIa, Q. 83, a. 4, c.

210 "Petit autem populus misericordiam quantum ad amotionem mali contra miseriam culpae et poenae, et pacem quantum ad consecutionem omnis boni; unde ter *agnus Dei*, dicitur." *In IV Sent.*, d. 8, ex.

211 *ST* IIIa, Q. 83, a. 5, obj. 7.

third, the distribution of graces proceeding from the Passion of Christ."[212]

St. Thomas spends the most time on the second of these three significations: the way in which the three pieces of the broken host correspond to three different groups within the Church, for which he invokes the authority of the Areopagite in the *Sentences*, and of Pope Sergius in the *Summa*.[213] First, the part of the host that gets consumed corresponds to those Christians who are still living on earth, since the living are united through receiving holy Communion — and because, like the consumed sacrament, they are "ground down," whether "by the passions" or "through diverse punishments," and this grinding is their means of incorporation into Christ, just as the sacrament's being

---

212 "Fractio hostiae tria significat, primo quidem, ipsam divisionem corporis Christi, quae facta est in passione; secundo, distinctionem corporis mystici secundum diversos status; tertio, distributionem gratiarum procedentium ex passione Christi, ut Dionysius dicit, III cap. Eccles. Hier. Unde talis fractio non inducit divisionem Christi." *ST* IIIa, Q. 83, a. 5, ad 7. In the *Scriptum*, St. Thomas combines the second and third significations here into a single item, and so he numbers only two significations in total. See *In IV Sent.*, d. 12, q. 1, a. 3, qa. 3: "Fractio duo significat, scilicet ipsam divisionem corporis veri, quae facta est in passione, . . . et distributionem virtutis redemptionis Christi per diversa membra ecclesiae."

213 "distributionem virtutis redemptionis Christi per diversa membra ecclesiae; et hanc significationem tangit Dionysius in 3 cap. *Eccl. Hierar.*" *In IV Sent.*, d. 12, q. 1, a. 3, qa. 3. "Sicut Sergius Papa dicit, et habetur in decretis, de Consecr., dist. II, *triforme est corpus domini.*" *ST* IIIa, Q. 83, a. 5, ad 8 (quoting *Decretum, de Consecratione*, d. 2, ch. 22).

ground down by the teeth is the means of its
recipient being united to Christ's body.[214] Second, the part of the host put into the chalice
corresponds to those who have already risen in
glory, not just spiritually but even bodily, like
Christ himself, his blessed Mother, "or if there
are any other saints who are with their bodies in
glory."[215] In this connection, St. Thomas quotes
Psalm 35:9: *They are inebriated by the bounty of
the house of God.*[216] Third and finally, there is
the part of the host that Pope Sergius identifies
as "still remaining on the altar until the end of
Mass" — although, St. Thomas notes, even by
his (Thomas's) time that practice has been dis-
continued.[217] Nevertheless, this third part was

---

214 "Quia quidam sunt adhuc vivi, et hi significantur
per partem quae comeditur: quia ipsi atteruntur diversis
poenalitatibus, et sunt in ipso motu, ut incorporentur
Christo." *In IV Sent.*, d. 12, q. 1, a. 3, qa. 3. "*Pars comesta
ambulans adhuc super terram*, quia scilicet viventes in terra
sacramento uniuntur; et passionibus conteruntur, sicut
panis comestus atteritur dentibus." *ST* IIIa, Q. 83, a. 5, ad 8.
215 "*Pars oblata in calicem missa corpus Christi quod iam
resurrexit, demonstrat*, scilicet ipsum Christum, et beatam
virginem, vel si qui alii sancti cum corporibus sunt in
gloria." *ST* IIIa, Q. 83, a. 5, ad 8.
216 "Quidam autem sunt mortui: et hi sunt in duplici
statu. Quia quidam in plena participatione beatitudinis;
et hoc est corpus Christi quod jam surrexit, sicut ipse
Christus, et Beata Virgo; et hi significantur per partem in
calice missam, quia *illi inebriantur ab ubertate domus Dei.*"
In IV Sent., d. 12, q. 1, a. 3, qa. 3.
217 "Hic tamen ritus non servatur modo, ut scilicet
una pars servetur usque in finem Missae. Manet tamen
eadem significatio partium." *ST* IIIa, Q. 83, a. 5, ad 8. Sev-
eral editions add the words "propter periculum" — namely

said to represent those who have died and are "in the expectation of full beatitude," whether the poor souls in Purgatory or the blessed souls in heaven, "for these pursue perfect glory unto the end of the world, and meanwhile they rest in appearances" — that is, *species*.[218] This is because that part of the host was meant to represent "the body of Christ remaining in the tomb," and so it was fitting to associate it with the bodies of the saints that "shall be in their tombs even until the end of the age."[219]

St. Thomas summarizes all of this with a helpful mnemonic device: *Hostia dividitur in partes, tincta beatos plene, sicca notat vivos, servata sepultos* — "The host is divided into parts: The intincted stands for those fully blessed, the dry for the living, the reserved for the buried" — which is more memorable in Latin than in English.[220] He also acknowledges, however, that not everyone agrees about these significations, and indeed some people even

---

"on account of the danger" to the Body of Christ left on the altar — but the Leonine Edition does not.

218 "Quidam autem sunt in expectatione plenae beatitudinis, qui vel stolam animae tantum habent, vel neutram, ut hi qui sunt in Purgatorio; et hi significantur per tertiam partem quae reservatur usque in finem: quia hi perfectam gloriam consequuntur in fine mundi, et interim in speciebus quiescunt." *In IV Sent.*, d. 12, q. 1, a. 3, qa. 3.

219 *"Pars in altari usque ad finem Missae remanens est corpus Christi in sepulcro remanens, quia usque in finem saeculi corpora sanctorum in sepulcris erunt*, quorum tamen animae sunt vel in Purgatorio vel in caelo." *ST* IIIa, Q. 83, a. 5, ad 8.

220 *ST* IIIa, Q. 83, a. 5, ad 8.

rotate the whole framework around, associating the part in the chalice with the living, the part reserved with the glorious, and the part consumed with the rest.[221] St. Thomas justifies this alternative schema by noting the two potential meanings of the chalice: On the one hand, the chalice represents the Passion, and so it makes sense that the piece inside would be for those who are still sharing in the sufferings of Christ; on the other hand, the chalice represents "the enjoyment of the blessed," and so it likewise makes sense that the piece inside would be for "those whose bodies are already in full beatitude."[222]

Here during the Fraction Rite, St. Thomas also points out the last signs of the cross that the priest will make over the consecrated species. And whereas the eight sets during the Canon corresponded to the Passion, this last group of three pertains instead to the Resurrection on the

---

221 "Quidam tamen dicunt quod pars in calicem missa significat eos qui vivunt in hoc mundo; pars autem extra calicem servata significat plene beatos quantum ad animam et corpus; pars autem comesta significat ceteros." *ST* IIIa, Q. 83, a. 5, ad 8.

222 "Per calicem duo possunt significari. Uno modo, ipsa passio, quae repraesentatur in hoc sacramento. Et secundum hoc, per partem in calicem missam significantur illi qui adhuc sunt participes passionum Christi. Alio modo, potest significari fruitio beata, quae etiam in hoc sacramento praefiguratur. Et ideo illi quorum corpora iam sunt in plena beatitudine, significantur per partem in calicem missam." *ST* IIIa, Q. 83, a. 5, ad 9.

third day.[223] In connection with the fraction, St. Thomas also makes an oblique argument against communion by intinction, and a striking one: "The part put into the chalice should not be given to the people as a supplement to communion, because Christ did not extend the intincted bread to anyone but Judas the betrayer."[224]

In the *Sentences* commentary, St. Thomas also mentions one last element of preparation for holy Communion. If the foregoing were all for the sake of preparing the entire people, the priest also has a special preparation for himself, namely his silent prayer that begins, *Domine Jesu Christe*.[225]

There follows the reception of holy Communion. This is done hierarchically, with the priest communicating himself first, and afterwards distributing the sacrament to others.[226]

---

223 "Nono autem, repraesentatur resurrectio tertia die facta, per tres cruces quae fiunt ad illa verba, *pax domini sit semper vobiscum*." *ST* IIIa, Q. 83, a. 5, ad 3. See also *In IV Sent.*, d. 12, ex: "Quia autem commixtio corporis et sanguinis unionem animae et corporis significat; ideo illa crucis signatio quae fit super illa verba: *pax Domini sit semper vobiscum*, magis pertinet ad resurrectionem, quae virtute Trinitatis et tertia die facta est."

224 "Et est notandum quod pars in calicem missa non debet populo dari in supplementum communionis, quia panem intinctum non porrexit Christus nisi Iudae proditori." *ST* IIIa, Q. 83, a. 5, ad 9.

225 "Praeparatio autem specialis sacerdotis sumentis fit per orationes quas privatim dicit, *Domine Jesu Christe*, et si quae aliae sunt." *In IV Sent.*, d. 8, ex.

226 "Deinde sequitur perceptio sacramenti, primo percipiente sacerdote, et postmodum aliis dante." *ST* IIIa, Q. 83, a. 4, c.

Thus St. Thomas recalls the teaching of the Areopagite in the *Ecclesiastical Hierarchy*: "He who hands on divine things to others, ought first to be a partaker himself."[227]

Whatever is left over of the blessed Sacrament is then reposed — concerning which there is an objection, namely that the reality should match the figure, but the paschal lamb, which is a figure of the holy Eucharist, had to be consumed all at once.[228] St. Thomas responds that this condition is sufficiently fulfilled by the fact that whatever hosts are consumed at that Mass are, like the paschal lamb, "not reserved until the next day."[229] He even quotes Pope Clement to show that the Church once forbade consecrating any more than would be received at that particular Mass: "But if any should remain," Clement had said, "let them not be reserved until the next day, but with fear and trembling let them be consumed by the diligence of the clerics."[230] However, St. Thomas notes, there is

---

227 "ut dicit Dionysius, III cap. Eccles. Hier., qui aliis divina tradit, primo debet ipse particeps esse." *ST* IIIa, Q. 83, a. 4, c. See also Denys, *Ecclesiastical Hierarchy*, Chapter 3, 445A.

228 *ST* IIIa, Q. 83, a. 5, obj. 11.

229 "Veritas quantum ad aliquid debet respondere figurae, quia scilicet non debet pars hostiae consecratae de qua sacerdos et ministri, vel etiam populus communicat, in crastinum reservari." *ST* IIIa, Q. 83, a. 5, ad 11.

230 "Unde, ut habetur de Consecr., dist. II, Clemens Papa statuit, *tanta holocausta in altario offerantur, quanta populo sufficere debeant. Quod si remanserint, in crastinum*

a key difference between this sacrament and the
paschal lamb, namely that "this sacrament must
be received daily, yet the paschal lamb was not
received daily."[231] Therefore, unlike with the
lamb in the Old Testament, now "it is necessary
to conserve other consecrated hosts for the sick,"
so that no one may die without the consolation
of Viaticum, and hence the necessity of repos-
ing whatever is left over.[232]

Following holy Communion, the priest undertakes the ablutions. Curiously, St. Thomas never
mentions the ablutions of the sacred vessels
in either *expositio Missae*: His concern is only
the purifying of the priest himself, specifically
his mouth and his fingers. The priest drinks
wine, a cleansing substance, in order "to cleanse
his mouth, lest any traces [of the sacrament]
should remain."[233] Like many before it, this
action is said to pertain "to reverence for the

---

non reserventur, sed cum timore et tremore clericorum diligentia
consumantur." *ST* IIIa, Q. 83, a. 5, ad 11.

231 ""Quia tamen hoc sacramentum quotidie sumendum est, non autem agnus paschalis quotidie sumebatur."
ST IIIa, Q. 83, a. 5, ad 11.

232 "Ideo oportet alias hostias consecratas pro infirmis
conservare. Unde in eadem distinctione legitur, *presbyter
Eucharistiam semper habeat paratam, ut, quando quis infirmatus fuerit, statim eum communicet, ne sine communione
moriatur.*" *ST* IIIa, Q. 83, a. 5, ad 11.

233 "Vinum, ratione suae humiditatis, est ablutivum.
Et ideo sumitur post perceptionem huius sacramenti, ad
abluendum os, ne aliquae reliquiae remaneant." *ST* IIIa,
Q. 83, a. 5, ad 10.

sacrament."[234] However, St. Thomas says, the priest does not do this if he is about to celebrate another Mass, since the "wine for the ablutions" would break his eucharistic fast for the next liturgy.[235] Having cleansed his mouth, the priest then "wets his fingers with wine," and this for the same reverential reason, since "with these fingers he had touched the body of Christ."[236]

THANKSGIVING (COMMUNION ANTIPHON–POSTCOMMUNION)

Finally we come to the very last section of the Mass, the Thanksgiving.[237] This part contains two things: the Communion antiphon, and the Postcommunion prayer. In fact, however, St. Thomas is under the impression that the Communion antiphon itself is intended as a kind of postcommunion, a looking back "after communion" in "remembrance of the benefit received," "with the people rejoicing for the reception of the mystery."[238] About the Post-

---

234 "quod pertinet ad reverentiam sacramenti." *ST* IIIa, Q. 83, a. 5, ad 10.

235 "Unde extra, de Celebrat. Miss., cap. ex parte, *sacerdos vino os perfundere debet postquam totum percepit sacramentum, nisi cum eodem die Missam aliam debuerit celebrare, ne, si forte vinum perfusionis acciperet, celebrationem aliam impediret.*" *ST* IIIa, Q. 83, a. 5, ad 10.

236 "Et eadem ratione perfundit vino digitos quibus corpus Christi tetigerat." *ST* IIIa, Q. 83, a. 5, ad 10.

237 "Ultimo autem tota Missae celebratio in gratiarum actione terminatur." *ST* IIIa, Q. 83, a. 4, c.

238 "rememorationem accepti beneficii in cantu antiphonae post communionem." *In IV Sent.*, d. 8, ex.

communion prayer, he says simply that it is the oration through which the priest gives thanks.[239] He also connects it to Christ's example on Holy Thursday, who, "when he had celebrated the supper with his disciples, said a hymn."[240] St. Thomas sees a harmonious symmetry between this ending of the Mass and its beginning, with the Communion and Post-communion reflecting the Introit and Collect, bringing the liturgy full circle.[241]

"On feast days," St. Thomas says, "the deacon dismisses the people at the end of the Mass, saying, *Ite missa est*."[242] And this, according to St. Thomas, may be one reason that the Mass is called the Mass, or *Missa*, in the first place. Of course, *missa* means "sent." And so St. Thomas interprets this dismissal to mean that, in the Mass, "Christ has been sent to us as host," and now that the Mass is finished, "the host has been sent to God through the angel" — recalling the angelic reference from

---

"populo exultante pro sumptione mysterii, quod significat cantus post communionem." *ST* IIIa, Q. 83, a. 4, c.

239 "gratiarum actionem in oratione, quam sacerdos prosequitur." *In IV Sent.*, d. 8, ex. "et sacerdote per orationem gratias offerente." *ST* IIIa, Q. 83, a. 4, c.

240 "sicut et Christus, celebrata cena cum discipulis, hymnum dixit, ut dicitur Matth. XXVI." *ST* IIIa, Q. 83, a. 4, c.

241 "ut conformiter finis Missae principio respondeat." *In IV Sent.*, d. 8, ex.

242 "Unde et in fine Missae diaconus in festis diebus populum licentiat, dicens, *ite, Missa est*." *ST* IIIa, Q. 83, a. 4, ad 9.

the Roman Canon.[243] In terms of the name
"Mass," however, St. Thomas considers a few
other possibilities for this nomenclature as well.
Perhaps it is not about Christ being sent as host,
but about Christ being sent as consecrator.[244]
Or maybe it is because "the priest sends prayers
to God through the angel, as the people [like-
wise] do through the priest."[245] Or it could be
because, when it comes time for the consecration, the deacon and the porter send out of the
church all the catechumens and those who are
not in communion.[246] Notably, in the *Scriptum*
St. Thomas does not connect his consideration
of the name "Mass" with the Ite at all, but only
in the *Summa*.[247]

---

243 "Vel quia Christus est hostia nobis missa." *ST* IIIa,
Q. 83, a. 4, ad 9. See also *In IV Sent.*, d. 13, ex: "Secundo
ipsa hostia sacra Missa vocari potest; quia transmissa est
prius a patre nobis, ut scilicet nobiscum esset, postea a
nobis patri, ut apud patrem pro nobis esset."

244 "Missa enim dicitur, eo quod caelestis missus
ad consecrandum vivificum corpus adveniat." *In IV Sent.*,
d. 13, ex (quoting Hugh of St. Victor).

245 "Et propter hoc etiam Missa nominatur. Quia per
Angelum sacerdos preces ad Deum mittit, sicut populus
per sacerdotem." *ST* IIIa, Q. 83, a. 4, ad 9. See also *In IV
Sent.*, d. 13, ex: "Primo, quia Missa dicitur quasi transmissa,
eo quod populus fidelis per ministerium sacerdotis, qui
mediatoris vice fungitur inter Deum et hominem, preces,
vota et oblationes Deo transmittit."

246 "Tertio Missa ab emittendo dicitur, ut quidam
dicunt; quia ut sacerdos hostiam consecrare incipit, per
manum diaconi et ostiarii catechumenos et non communicantes foras ecclesiam mittit." *In IV Sent.*, d. 13, ex.

247 See *In IV Sent.*, d. 13, ex; and *ST* IIIa, Q. 83, a.
4, ad 9.

By way of epilogue, or grand finale, St. Thomas Aquinas ends his *expositio Missae* in the *Sentences* commentary with a reflection on the different languages used in the Mass. Some words in the Mass are in Greek — for example, "*Kyrie eleison*, 'Lord have mercy.'"[248] Others are in Hebrew — "such as *Alleluia*, 'Praise God'; *Sabaoth*, 'hosts'; *Hosanna*, 'Save, I beg'; *Amen*, 'Truly' or 'Let it be done.'"[249] Most of the rest of the Mass, obviously, is in Latin.[250] St. Thomas teaches that the combination of these three languages in the liturgy — Greek, Hebrew, and Latin — is beautifully fitting. For as we have seen many times in this study, the Mass is a representation of Christ's Passion — and of course, "the titulus of the cross of Christ was written in these three languages."[251]

---

248 "Sciendum autem, quod in officio Missae, ubi passio repraesentatur, quaedam continentur verba Graeca, sicut, *kyrie eleison*, idest Domine miserere." *In IV Sent.*, d. 8, ex.

249 "quaedam Hebraica, sicut *alleluja*, idest laudate Deum; *Sabaoth*, idest exercituum; *hosanna*, salva obsecro; *amen*, idest vere, vel fiat." *In IV Sent.*, d. 8, ex.

250 "quaedam Latina, quae patent." *In IV Sent.*, d. 8, ex.

251 "in officio Missae, ubi passio repraesentatur . . . quia his tribus linguis scriptus est titulus crucis Christi, Joan. 19." *In IV Sent.*, d. 8, ex.

CONCLUSION

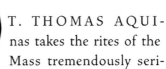

T. THOMAS AQUI-
nas takes the rites of the
Mass tremendously seri-
ously. In fact, so great is his respect for these
sacred rites that he believes that any celebrant
who deviates from them should be threatened
with the loss of his priestly office—to say nothing of the grave spiritual danger in which such
a minister places himself.[1] In the *sed contra* of
our *Tertia Pars*, Question 83, Article 4, in defense
of the words of the Mass, St. Thomas quotes a
text from Gratian as saying, "James the brother

---

1 "Aliter celebrare dicitur qui non servat materiam
vel formam aut ritum debitum ab ecclesia institutum; et
debet talis, si ex contemptu faciat, gradus sui periculo
subjacere." *In IV Sent.*, d. 12, ex. See also *ST* IIIa, Q. 83, a.
3, ad 8: "Si sacerdos verba consecrationis proferat super
materia debita cum intentione consecrandi, absque omnibus praedictis, scilicet domo et altari, calice et corporali
consecratis, et ceteris huiusmodi per Ecclesiam institutis,
consecrat quidem in rei veritate corpus Christi, peccat
tamen graviter, ritum Ecclesiae non servans."

of the Lord according to the flesh, and Basil the bishop of Caesarea, edited the celebration of the Mass"—"from whose authority," St. Thomas continues, "it is clear that each and every thing [said] around this [sacrament] is said fittingly."[2] Then in the *sed contra* of Article 5, against various objections that the actions of the Mass are unfitting, he simply says, "But to the contrary is the custom of the Church, who cannot err, as she is instructed by the Holy Spirit."[3] Thus St. Thomas understands the words and actions of the eucharistic liturgy to have been handed down on the authority of the apostles, the Fathers, the Church, and, indeed, God himself.[4]

This book has examined the rich meaning that St. Thomas attributes to each of these liturgical words and actions. My hope is that it might serve as a foundation for further studies as well. One such study could take up the liturgical topics of the other articles in this *Tertia*

---

2 "Sed contra est quod dicitur de Consecr., dist. I, *Iacobus frater domini secundum carnem, et Basilius Caesariensis episcopus, ediderunt Missae celebrationem.* Ex quorum auctoritate patet convenienter singula circa hoc dici." *ST* IIIa, Q. 83, a. 4, sc (quoting *Decretum, de Consecratione,* d. 1, ch. 47; which is itself quoting canon 32 of the Quinisext Council).

3 "Sed in contrarium est Ecclesiae consuetudo, quae errare non potest, utpote spiritu sancto instructa." *ST* IIIa, Q. 83, a. 5, sc.

4 In terms of the patristic authority of the liturgy, St. Thomas often cites texts of the Mass, but then names this source not as the missal, but as St. Gregory the Great, so closely does he associate the two. See, for example, *In II Sent.,* d. 36, q. 1, a. 4, sc 1; and *Super Ephesios* 2, l. 2.

Pars, Question 83: the proper time and place for holy Mass (Articles 2 and 3 respectively), and what to do if things go awry in its celebration (Article 6) — once again weaving these together with St. Thomas's earlier work in the *Scriptum* on the *Sentences*. Another study could consider St. Thomas's theology of the other six sacraments and their rites, supplementing the *Sentences* with the *Summa Contra Gentiles* for those sacraments not covered in the *Summa Theologiae*. It would also be useful to trace St. Thomas's various mystagogical sources — including Denys the Areopagite, Amalarius of Metz, Hugh of St. Victor, and Pope Innocent III — to better understand how Thomas is setting them in order in these *expositiones Missae*, and where, if anywhere, he is being original. A related question is precisely which missal St. Thomas had in mind when composing these texts.[5] One could also

---

5 A few observations that may be salient: St. Thomas refers to the opening chant as the Introit rather than as the Officium. He does not indicate separate oblations for the two species at the Offertory. He alludes to the cruciform extension of the arms at the Unde et Memores. He comments on a version of the Fraction Rite that he admits is already obsolete in his day. It may be that St. Thomas is trying to offer a commentary on the rites of the Mass in general, abstracting, at least for the most part, from the details that would distinguish one missal from another. It could also be that he is commenting on the Mass simply as it is handed down in the tradition of the *expositiones Missae*, rather than as celebrated anywhere in particular in the thirteenth century. See also Rasmussen, "Saint Thomas et les rites de la Messe," 27–28.

profitably compare St. Thomas's treatment of
the rites of the Mass with the treatments of his
contemporaries, especially his teacher St. Albert
the Great, and William Durandus. Another work
could compare St. Thomas with liturgical com-
mentators in other ages, including the Fathers of
the Church, as well as prominent figures of the
Liturgical Movement in the first half of the twen-
tieth century, to evaluate whether their projects
are essentially the same as that of St. Thomas,
or whether the scholastic *expositio Missae* is
something fundamentally distinct from what
preceded and followed after. Finally, it would be
worthwhile to put St. Thomas into conversation
with *Sacrosanctum Concilium*, and then especially
with the reformers of the liturgy in the period
following the Second Vatican Council.

In his scholastic mystagogy, St. Thomas Aquinas reads the Mass in a way analogous to how
he reads the sacred scriptures: First he considers the rite itself, then the deeper significance
hiding within it, which opens up for those who
seek with faith. Like all the best things, the
Mass is hard for us to understand.[6] Its texts
are hieratic and exotic and often inaudible, its
movements hierarchical and ritualized and often

---

6 Following Aristotle, St. Thomas teaches that the
order of knowing is the inverse of the order of being, such
that what is best and most knowable in itself is the least
knowable to us, because of the weakness of our intellects.
See, for example, *Super De Trinitate*, Ch. 1, Q. 1, a. 3.

invisible. In recent years, we have seen many
liturgists try to solve for this difficulty, by calling
for the Mass to be simplified, made transpar-
ent and plain, and translated into an everyday
idiom. But if the mystical meaning of the Mass
is something like the spiritual sense of sacred
scripture, then on St. Thomas Aquinas's principles, this push for vulgarization is a terrible
mistake. It would be like replacing the inspired
word of God — which is often similarly difficult
and obscure — with a children's picture Bible.
Whereas for St. Thomas, the scriptures are difficult by design, not only because the richness of
the form should fit the richness of the content,
but also because an easier text would not hold
our attention anyway.[7] St. Thomas's *expositiones
Missae* suggest that the same logic applies to the
rites of the Mass. It is not a mistake that the
liturgy is mysterious — it unveils precisely by

---

7 "Utiliter est a Deo dispositum ut veritas in sacra
Scriptura cum aliqua difficultate manifestetur." *Quodlibet
VII*, Q. 6, a. 1, ad 2. Of course this is not to advocate for
an absolute obscurantism. It is not that the liturgy must
be difficult through and through, but only that, where
it is difficult, this should be understood as a feature
and not a bug, just as with sacred scripture. For as St.
Thomas's reply to the very next objection explains, "As
Augustine says in *On Christian Doctrine*, there is nothing
which is handed over secretly in some place of sacred
Scripture, 'which elsewhere is not' expounded clearly."
("Sicut dicit Augustinus, De doctrina Christiana, nihil
est quod occulte in aliquo loco sacrae Scripturae trada-
tur, *quod non alibi* manifeste exponatur.") *Quodlibet VII*,
Q. 6, a. 1, ad 3.

veiling.[8] After the example of St. Thomas, the right response to the difficulty of understanding the Mass is not to dispel the difficulty, to dispel the mystery, but to contemplate it. Perhaps, therefore, the best way to read St. Thomas Aquinas's theology of the rites of the Mass, is as a liturgical *lectio divina*.

---

8 See *ST* Ia, Q. 1, a. 9, c (quoting Denys, *Celestial Hierarchy*, Chapter 1, 121B–C): "Impossibile est nobis aliter lucere divinum radium, nisi varietate sacrorum velaminum circumvelatum." This text is not about the liturgy in particular, but about divine manifestation in general, but the entirety of the *Ecclesiastical Hierarchy* shows how it can be applied to the sacred liturgy.

The Texts of St. Thomas
(LATIN AND ENGLISH)

In IV Sent., D. 8, EX.

. . .[†] *Per reliqua autem omnia quae dicuntur, laus Deo defertur.* Sciendum, quod eorum quae in officio Missae dicuntur, quaedam dicuntur per sacerdotem, quaedam per ministros, quaedam a toto choro. Ea quidem quibus populus immediate ordinatur ad Deum, per sacerdotes tantum dicuntur, qui sunt mediatores inter populum et Deum; quorum quaedam dicuntur publice, spectantia ad totum populum, in cujus persona ipse solus ea Deo proponit, sicut orationes et gratiarum actiones; quaedam privatim, quae ad officium ipsius tantum spectant, ut consecrationes et hujusmodi orationes quas ipse pro populo facit, non tamen in persona populi orans; et in omnibus praemittit: *Dominus vobiscum*, ut mens populi Deo conjungatur ad ipsum per intentionem erecti. Et quia populus in his quae ad Deum sunt, sacerdotem ducem habet, ideo in fine cujuslibet orationis populus consentit respondens: *amen*; unde et omnis sacerdotis oratio alte terminatur, etiam si privatim fiat. Ad ea vero quae per ministerium aliorum divinitus sunt tradita,

---

[†] St. Thomas had treated a few other things in this *expositio textus* before beginning his commentary on the words of the Mass — namely the order of the sacraments of initiation, the order between the sacraments in the law of nature and the sacraments of the Old Law and the sacraments of the New Law, and why Peter Lombard, and St. Ambrose before him, do not quote the form of the sacrament precisely. Interesting though those topics be, it seemed better to restrict ourselves to the topic at hand, and to omit those other discussions, beginning instead from the beginning of the *expositio Missae*.

In IV Sent., D. 8, EX.

..."Yet through everything else that is said, praise is offered to God." It must be known that, of those things that are said in the office of the Mass, some are said by the priest, some by the ministers, and some by the whole choir. Those things indeed by which the people is immediately ordered to God, are said only by priests, who are the mediators between the people and God; of which some are said publicly, regarding the whole people, in whose person the priest alone offers them to God, such as prayers and thanksgivings; some privately, which regard only the priest's own office, like consecrations and prayers of this sort that he makes for the people, nevertheless not praying in the person of the people; and before all of these, public or private, he first says, *Dominus vobiscum*, so that the minds of the people, raised up to him through their attention, might be joined to God. And because the people have the priest as their leader in these things that are unto God, at the end of every prayer the people consent, responding, *Amen*; whence also every prayer of the priest is ended out-loud, even if it is said privately. Whereas to those things that are handed down from above through the ministry of others, the people are ordered through the ministers of the altar. Whereas those that pertain to the disposing of the people, the choir undertakes: of which some are begun by the priest, which pertain to those things that exceed human reason, as though received from above; some the choir says itself,

per ministros altaris populus ordinatur. Ea vero quae
ad dispositionem populi pertinent, chorus prosequitur:
quorum quaedam a sacerdote inchoantur, quae ad ea
pertinent quae rationem humanam excedunt, quasi
divinitus accepta: quaedam chorus per seipsum, quibus
illa declarantur quae rationi sunt consona. Item quaedam pertinent ad populum ut praeparatoria ad divina
percipienda; et haec a choro praemittuntur his quae a
ministris et sacerdote dicuntur; quaedam vero ex perceptione divinorum in populo causata; et haec sequuntur.
His ergo visis, sciendum est, quod quia omnis nostra
operatio a Deo inchoata, circulariter in ipsum terminari
debet; ideo Missae officium incipit ab oratione, et terminatur in gratiarum actione. Unde tres habet partes
principales; scilicet principium orationis quod durat
usque ad epistolam; medium celebrationem ipsam quae
durat usque ad postcommunionem; et finem gratiarum
actionis exinde usque in finem.

Prima pars duo continet; scilicet populi praeparationem
ad orationem, et ipsam orationem. Praeparatur autem
populus ad orationem tripliciter. Primo per devotionem,
quae excitatur in introitu; unde et sumitur ex aliquo
pertinente ad solemnitatem, in cujus devotionem populus congregatur, et etiam adjungitur Psalmus. Secundo
humilitatem, quae fit per *kyrie eleison*, quia misericordiam
petens miseriam profitetur; et dicitur novies propter
novem choros angelorum, vel propter fidem Trinitatis,
secundum quod quaelibet persona in se consideratur et
in ordine ad alias duas. Tertio per rectam intentionem,
quae ad caelestem patriam et gloriam dirigenda est, quae
omnem rationem humanam excedit; et hoc fit per *gloria
in excelsis*, quam chorus prosequitur sacerdote inchoante;
et ideo non dicitur nisi in solemnitatibus quae nobis

namely those by which those things are proclaimed that are consonant with reason. Likewise some pertain to the people as preparatory for receiving divine things, and these are said by the choir before those that are said by the ministers and the priest; whereas some pertain to the people as caused by the people's reception of divine things, and these follow after the things said by the priest and ministers. With these things having been seen, therefore, it must be known that, because every operation of ours is begun by God, so it ought to be terminated in him, coming full circle. Thus the office of the Mass begins with prayer, and is terminated in thanksgiving. Whence it has three principal parts: namely the beginning of prayer which lasts until the Epistle; the celebration itself in the middle that lasts until the Postcommunion; and the end of thanksgiving then lasts from there until the end.

The first part contains two things: namely the preparation of the people for prayer, and the prayer itself. Yet the people are prepared for prayer in three ways. First through devotion, which is excited in the Introit; whence also it is taken from something pertaining to the solemnity, in the devotion to which the people are gathered, and also a Psalm is added. Second through humility, which is done through the Kyrie Eleison, because the one seeking mercy declares his misery; and it is said nine times on account of the nine choirs of angels, or on account of the faith of the Trinity, according as each person is considered in himself and in order to the other two. Third through right intention, which must be directed to the heavenly fatherland and glory, which exceeds all human reason; and this is done through the

caelestem solemnitatem repraesentant; in officiis vero luctus omnino intermittitur. Deinde sequitur oratio ad Deum pro populo fusa, quam sacerdos publice proponit praemisso *Dominus vobiscum*, quod sumitur de Ruth 2. Pontifex autem dicit: *pax vobis*, gerens typum Christi qui his verbis discipulos post resurrectionem allocutus est, Joan. 20.

Secunda autem pars principalis tres partes continet. Prima est populi instructio usque ad offertorium; secunda, materiae oblatio usque ad praefationem; tertia, sacramenti consummatio usque ad post communionem. Instructio autem populi fit per verbum Dei, quod quidem a Deo per ministros suos ad populum pervenit; et ideo ea quae ad instructionem plebis pertinent, non dicuntur a sacerdote, sed a ministris.

Ministerium autem verbi Dei est triplex. Primum auctoritatis, quod competit Christo qui dicitur *minister*, Rom. 15, de quo dicitur Matth. 7, 29: *erat autem in potestate docens*. Secundum manifestae veritatis quae competit praedicatoribus novi testamenti, de quo dicitur 2 Corinth. 3, 6: *qui et idoneos nos fecit ministros*, etc. Tertium figurationis, quod competit praedicatoribus veteris testamenti; et ideo doctrinam Christi proponit diaconus. Et quia Christus non solum est homo, sed Deus; ideo diaconus praemittit: *Dominus vobiscum*, ut ad Christum quasi ad Deum homines attentos faciat. Doctrina vero praedicatorum novi testamenti proponitur per subdiaconos. Nec obstat quod aliquando ab eis legitur loco

Gloria in Excelsis, which the choir completes with the priest beginning it; and thus it is not said except on solemnities that represent heavenly solemnity to us; whereas in offices of mourning it is omitted completely. Then there follows the prayer to God poured forth for the people, which the priest proclaims publicly, introduced by *Dominus vobiscum*, which is taken from Ruth 2. Yet a bishop says, *Pax vobis*, bearing the type of Christ who addressed the disciples with these words after the Resurrection, in John 20:19.

Yet the second principal part contains three parts. The first is the Instruction of the people until the Offertory; the second, the Oblation of the matter until the Preface; the third, the consummation of the sacrament until the Postcommunion. Yet the Instruction of the people is done through the word of God, which indeed came to the people from God through his ministers; and thus those things that pertain to the instruction of the people, are not said by the priest, but by the ministers.

Yet the ministry of the word of God is threefold. First of authority, which applies to Christ who is called *minister* in Romans 15, of whom it is said in Matthew 7:29: *Yet he was teaching in power*. Second of manifest truth, which applies to the preachers of the New Testament, of whom it is said in 2 Corinthians 3:6: *who also made us worthy ministers*, etc. Third of prefiguration, which applies to the preachers of the Old Testament; and thus a deacon proclaims the teaching of Christ. And because Christ is not only man, but also God, thus the deacon introduces the Gospel with *Dominus vobiscum*, so that he might make men attentive to Christ as God. Whereas the teaching of the preachers of the New Testament is proclaimed by

epistolae aliquid de veteri testamento, quia praedicatores novi testamenti etiam vetus praedicant. Doctrina
vero praedicatorum veteris testamenti per inferiores
ministros legitur non semper, sed illis diebus quibus
praecipue configuratio novi et veteris testamenti designatur, ut in jejuniis quatuor temporum, et quando
aliqua celebrantur quae in veteri lege figurata sunt, sicut
passio, nativitas, baptismus, et aliquod hujusmodi. Et
quia utraque doctrina ordinat ad Christum, et eorum
qui praeibant, et eorum qui sequebantur; ideo doctrina
Christi postponitur quasi finis.

Ex doctrina autem ordinante ad Christum duplex effectus populo provenit, quibus etiam homo praeparatur ad
doctrinam Christi: scilicet profectus virtutum, qui per
graduale insinuatur: dicitur enim a gradu quo ascenditur
de virtute in virtutem, vel a gradibus altaris ante quos
dicitur; et exultatio habita de aeternorum spe, quod
insinuat *alleluja*; unde et replicatur propter stolam animae et corporis. In diebus vero et officiis luctus intermittitur, et loco ejus, tractus ponitur, qui asperitate vocum
et prolixitate verborum praesentis miseriae incolatum
insinuat. Tempore autem resurrectionis duplex *alleluja*
dicitur propter gaudium resurrectionis capitis, et membrorum. Effectus autem evangelicae doctrinae est fidei
confessio; quae quia supra rationem est, a sacerdote
inchoatur symbolum fidei et chorus prosequitur, nec
dicitur nisi in illis solemnitatibus de quibus fit mentio in
symbolo, sicut de nativitate, resurrectione, de apostolis,
qui fidei fundatores extiterunt, ut dicitur 1 Corinth. 3,
10: *ut sapiens architectus fundamentum posui.*

subdeacons. Nor is it wrong that sometimes in place of
the Epistle something from the Old Testament is read by
them, because the preachers of the New Testament also
preach the Old. Whereas the teaching of the preachers
of the Old Testament is read by inferior ministers — not
always, but on those days when the configuration of the
New and Old Testaments is especially indicated, such as
on the Ember Day fasts, and when various things are
celebrated that are prefigured in the Old Law, like the
Passion, the Nativity, the Baptism, and whatever else
of this sort. And because both of these teachings are
ordered to Christ, both the teaching of those who went
before him, and that of those who followed after him,
thus the teaching of Christ is proclaimed at the end.

Yet from the teaching that orders one to Christ, a
twofold effect arises for the people, by which man is
also prepared for the teaching of Christ: namely an
advancement of the virtues, which is suggested by the
Gradual: for this name is taken from the grade or step
by which one ascends from virtue to virtue, or from
the steps of the altar before which it is said; and the
exultation that comes from the hope of eternal things,
which the Alleluia suggests, whence also it is repeated
on account of the stole of the soul and the stole of the
body. Whereas on days and in offices of mourning it
is omitted, and in its place there is put a Tract, which,
by the harshness of the voices and the prolixity of the
words, suggests the exile of present misery. Yet in the
time of the Resurrection, a double Alleluia is said, on
account of the joy of the Resurrection, of the head and
of the members. Yet the effect of the Gospel teaching is
the confession of the faith; which, because it is above
reason, the Symbol of Faith is begun by the priest and

Deinde sequitur secunda pars partis secundae principalis quae pertinet ad materiae consecrandae oblationem; et hic tria continentur. Praemittitur enim offerentium exultatio, quasi praeparatoria, in offertorio, quia *hilarem datorem diligit Deus*, 2 Corinth. 9, 7: exprimitur ipsa oblatio dum dicitur: *suscipe sancta Trinitas*: petitur oblationis acceptatio per orationes secreto dictas, quia hoc sacerdotis tantum est Deum oblationibus placare: ad quam orationem sacerdos per humiliationem se praeparat dicens: *in spiritu humilitatis et in animo contrito suscipiamur a te Domine*. Et quia haec tria praedicta exigunt mentis erectionem ad Deum, ideo omnibus tribus praemittitur: *Dominus vobiscum*, loco cujus quando oratio secreta facienda est, dicitur: *orate fratres*.

Tertia pars secundae principalis partis, quae ad sacramenti perceptionem pertinet, tria continet. Primo praeparationem; secundo sacramenti perfectionem, ibi: *te igitur* etc., tertio sacramenti sumptionem, ibi: *oremus. Praeceptis salutaribus moniti, et divina institutione formati audemus dicere*. Praeparatio autem populi et ministrorum et sacerdotis ad tantum sacramentum fit per devotam Dei laudem; unde in praefatione, in qua fit dicta praeparatio, tria continentur. Primo populi excitatio ad laudem, ubi sacerdos praemisso *Dominus vobiscum*, quod ad totam hanc tertiam partem referendum est,

the choir follows, nor is it said except on those solemnities of which mention is made in the Symbol, as of the
Nativity, the Resurrection, the Apostles, who were the
founders of the faith, as is said in 1 Corinthians 3:10:
as a wise architect put the foundation.

Then there follows the second part of the second principal part, which pertains to the Oblation of the matter
to be consecrated; and here three things are contained.
For the exultation of those offering comes first, as preparatory, in the Offertory, because *God loves a cheerful
giver* (2 Corinthians 9:7); the Oblation itself is expressed
when he says, *Suscipe sancta Trinitas*; the acceptance of
the Oblation is begged through the prayers said secretly,
because it belongs to the priest alone to placate God
with oblations: for which prayer the priest prepares
himself through humiliation, saying, *In spiritu humilitatis
et in animo contrito suscipiamur a te Domine*. And because
these three aforementioned things require the lifting up
of the mind to God, thus there is set before all three
Dominus vobiscum, in place of which, when the Secret
prayer must be said, there is said, *Orate fratres*.

The third part of the second principal part, which
pertains to the reception [*perceptio*] of the sacrament,
contains three things. First preparation; second the
completion of the sacrament, at *Te igitur* etc.; third
the reception of the sacrament, at *Oremus. Praeceptis
salutaribus moniti, et divina institutione formati audemus
dicere*. Yet the preparation of the people and ministers
and priest for so great a sacrament is done through the
devout praise of God; whence in the Preface, in which
the aforementioned preparation is made, three things
are contained. First, the arousal of the people to praise,

inducit ad mentis erectionem, dicens: *sursum corda*, et
ad gratiarum actionem, dicens: *gratias agamus Domino
Deo nostro.* Secundo Deum implorat ad laudem suscipiendum, ostendens laudis debitum, dicens: *vere dignum*,
ratione Dominii (unde subdit: *Domine sancte); justum*
ratione paternitatis (unde subdit: *pater omnipotens);*
aequum, ratione deitatis (unde subdit: *aeterne Deus);*
salutare, ratione redemptionis (unde subdit: *per Christum
Dominum nostrum*). Quandoque vero adjungitur aliqua
alia laudis materia secundum congruentiam solemnitatis,
sicut: *et te in assumptione Beatae Mariae semper Virginis
collaudare;* etiam proponens laudis exemplum: *per quem
majestatem tuam laudant angeli.* Tertio populus laudes
exsolvit divinitatis, assumens angelorum verba: *sanctus,
sanctus, sanctus Dominus Deus exercituum*, Isa. 6, 3, et
humanitatis Christi, assumens verba puerorum, Matth.
21, 10: *benedictus qui venit in nomine Domini.*

Illa autem pars quae perfectionem sacramenti continet,
in tres dividitur, secundum tria quae sunt de integritate
hujus sacramenti: scilicet aliquid quod est sacramentum
tantum; aliquid quod est res et sacramentum; aliquid
quod est res tantum. In prima ergo parte continetur benedictio oblatae materiae, quae est tantum sacramentum;
in secunda corporis et sanguinis Christi consecratio,
quod est res et sacramentum, ibi: *quam oblationem;* in
tertia, effectus sacramenti postulatio quod est res tantum,
ibi: *supra quae propitio ac sereno vultu respicere digneris.*
Circa primum duo facit sacerdos: primo petit oblationis

when the priest, having said *Dominus vobiscum* (which must be referred to this whole third part), spurs them to the lifting up of the mind, saying, *Sursum corda*, and to thanksgiving, saying, *Gratias agamus Domino Deo nostro*. Second, he implores God to receive the praise, showing that praise is due, saying, *vere dignum* [truly worthy or right], by reason of his dominion (whence he adds, *Domine sancte*); *justum* [just] by reason of his paternity (whence he adds, *Pater omnipotens*); *aequum* [fair], by reason of his deity (whence he adds, *aeterne Deus*); *salutare* [salvific], by reason of the redemption (whence he adds, *per Christum Dominum nostrum*). Whereas sometimes there is included some other matter of praise according to what befits the solemnity, such as: *et te in assumptione Beatae Mariae semper Virginis collaudare*; also setting forth the example of praise: *per quem majestatem tuam laudant angeli*. Third, the people break forth in the praises of the divinity, taking up the words of the angels: *Sanctus, sanctus, sanctus Dominus Deus exercituum*, from Isaiah 6:3; and of the humanity of Christ, taking up the words of the children in Matthew 21:10: *benedictus qui venit in nomine Domini*.

Yet that part which contains the completion of the sacrament is divided into three, according to the three things that belong to the integrity of this sacrament: namely something that is the *sacramentum tantum*; something that is the *res et sacramentum*; and something that is the *res tantum*. Therefore in the first part there is contained the blessing of the matter offered, which is the *sacramentum tantum*; in the second there is the consecration of the body and blood of Christ, which is the *res et sacramentum*, at *Quam oblationem*; in the third, the petition for the effect of the sacrament, which is the

benedictionem, quae dicitur *donum* a Deo nobis datum, *munus* Deo a nobis oblatum, *sacrificium* ad nostram salutem a Deo sanctificatum; secundo petit *offerentibus*, sive pro quibus offertur, salutem, ibi: *in primis quae tibi offerimus*, etc.

Ubi tria facit: primo commemorat eos pro quorum utilitate offertur hostia tam quantum ad generalem statum ecclesiae, quam quantum ad personas speciales, ibi: *memento*; secundo commemorat eos in quorum offertur reverentia, ibi: *communicantes*; et ponitur Virgo quae Christum in templo obtulit, apostoli qui ritum offerendi nobis tradiderunt, et martyres qui seipsos Deo obtulerunt, non autem confessores, quia de eis antiquitus non solemnizabat ecclesia, vel quia non sunt passi sicut Christus, cujus passionis memoriale est hoc sacramentum: tertio concluditur expresse quid per oblationem hostiae impetrandum petatur, ibi: *hanc igitur oblationem*, etc.

Quam oblationem, etc. Haec pars ad consecrationem pertinet, quae tria continet: primo imploratur consecrantis virtus; secundo perficitur consecratio, ibi: *qui pridie quam pateretur, accepit panem*; tertio exponitur rei consecratae commemoratio, ibi: *unde et memores*, etc. Verba autem illa quae ibi dicuntur: *benedictam, adscriptam, ratam, rationabilem, acceptabilemque*, possunt referri uno modo ad hoc quod est res contenta in hoc sacramento, scilicet Christum, qui est hostia benedicta ab omni macula peccati immunis; adscripta, idest praefigurata

res tantum, at *Supra quae propitio ac sereno vultu respicere digneris*. About the first the priest does two things: first he asks for the blessing of the Oblation, which is called a *donum* [gift] given to us by God, a *munus* [offering] offered to God by us, a *sacrificium* [sacrifice] sanctified by God for our salvation; second, he asks for salvation for the *offerentibus* [those offering], or those for whom it is offered, at *In primis quae tibi offerimus*, etc.

Here he does three things: first, he commemorates those for whose benefit the host is offered, both as regards the general state of the Church, and as regards special persons, at *Memento*; second, he commemorates those in whose reverence it is offered, at *Communicantes*, and there is placed the Virgin who offered Christ in the temple, the apostles who handed on the rite of offering to us, and the martyrs who offered themselves to God, yet not confessors, because the ancient Church did not celebrate them, or because they did not suffer like Christ, of whose Passion this sacrament is the memorial; third, what is sought to be obtained through the Oblation of the host is expressly concluded, at *Hanc igitur oblationem*, etc.

Quam oblationem, etc. This part pertains to the consecration, which contains three things: first, the power of the one consecrating is implored; second, the consecration is completed, at *Qui pridie quam pateretur, accepit panem*; third, there is expounded the commemoration of the thing consecrated, at *Unde et memores* etc. Yet those words that are said there — *benedictam, adscriptam, ratam, rationabilem, acceptabilemque* — can be referred in one way to the thing contained in this sacrament, namely Christ, who is the *benedictam* [blessed] host,

figuris veteris testamenti, et praedestinatione divina praeordinata; rata, quia non transitoria; rationabilis, propter congruitatem ad placandum; acceptabilis, propter efficaciam. Alio modo possunt referri ad ipsam hostiam, quae est sacramentum tantum; quam petit fieri *benedictam*, ut Deus eam consecret; sed ut confirmet quantum ad memoriam: *adscriptam*; quantum ad propositum immobile: *ratam*; ut eam acceptet: *rationabilem*, quantum ad judicium rationis; *acceptabilem*, quantum ad beneplacitum voluntatis. Tertio modo possunt referri ad effectum; unde dicit, *benedictam*, per quam benedicimur; *adscriptam*, per quam in caelis ascribamur; *ratam*, per quam in membris Christi censeamur; *rationabilem*, per quam a bestiali sensu eruamur; *acceptabilem*, per quam Deo accepti simus.

Supra quae propitio ac sereno vultu respicere digneris. Hic petit sacerdos sacramenti effectum; et primo effectum gratiae; secundo effectum gloriae, ibi: *memento etiam Domine famulorum famularumque tuarum.* Circa primum duo facit: primo petit acceptari sacramentum, quod est gratiae causa; secundo petit dari gratiae donum, ibi: *supplices te rogamus*; cujus expositio infra, dist. 13, ponetur. Effectum autem gloriae primo petit jam mortuis, ibi, *memento*, secundo adhuc vivis, ibi: *nobis quoque peccatoribus.* Completur autem canon Missae more aliarum orationum in Christo, ibi: *per Christum Dominum nostrum*, per quem hoc sacramentum originem habet et quantum ad substantiam; unde dicit, *creas* propter esse

immune to every stain of sin; *adscriptam* [reckoned],
that is, prefigured by the figures of the Old Testament,
and preordained by divine predestination; *ratam* [fixed],
because not transitory; *rationabilem* [reasonable], on
account of its fittingness for placating; *acceptabilem*
[acceptable], on account of its efficacy. In another way,
these words can be referred to the host itself, which
is the *sacramentum tantum*, the sacrament only; which
he asks to be made *benedictam*, so that God would
consecrate it; but to confirm it as regards memory:
adscriptam; immovable as regards purpose: *ratam*; so
that he might accept it: *rationabilem*, as regards the
judgment of reason; *acceptabilem*, as regards the pleasure of the will. In a third way they can be referred to
the effect; whence he says, *benedictam*, through which
we are blessed; *adscriptam*, through which we may be
enrolled in heaven; *ratam*, through which we may be
counted among Christ's members; *rationabilem*, through
which we may be saved from bestial sense; *acceptabilem*,
through which we may be welcome before God.

Supra quae propitio ac sereno vultu respicere digneris. Here
the priest asks for the effect of the sacrament; and first
the effect of grace; second the effect of glory, at *Memento
etiam Domine famulorum famularumque tuarum.* About the
first, he does two things: first, he asks that the sacrament, which is the cause of grace, be accepted; second,
he asks that the gift of grace be given, at *Supplices te
rogamus*; the exposition of which is put below in Distinction 13. Yet he asks for the effect of glory first for
those already dead, at *Memento*, second for those still
living, at *Nobis quoque peccatoribus.* Yet the Canon of the
Mass is completed, after the custom of other prayers,
in Christ, at *Per Christum Dominum nostrum*, through

naturae; *sanctificas*, propter esse sacramenti: et quantum ad virtutem; unde dicit, *vivificas*, propter effectum gratiae, quae est vita animae; *benedicis*, propter gratiae augmentum; et quantum ad operationem, sive usum; unde dicit: *et praestas nobis*.

Oremus. Praeceptis salutaribus moniti, et divina institutione formati audemus dicere. Hic ponitur sacramenti perceptio, ad quam praemittitur praeparatio communis et specialis. Communis triplex: primo enim ponitur sacramenti petitio in oratione Dominica, in qua dicitur: *panem nostrum quotidianum da nobis hodie*; secundo percipientium expiatio per orationem sacerdotis: *libera nos*; tertio pacis adimpletio, ibi: *pax Domini*. Hoc enim sacramentum est sanctitatis et pacis; et quia pax Christi exsuperat omnem sensum, ideo pacis petitio a sacerdote inchoatur, cum dicit *pax Domini*, et a choro completur, cum dicitur, *agnus Dei*; et sic tria a sacerdote incepta prosequitur, scilicet, *gloria in excelsis*, quod pertinet ad spem; *credo in unum Deum*, quod pertinet ad fidem; *pax Domini*, quod pertinet ad caritatem. Petit autem populus misericordiam quantum ad amotionem mali contra miseriam culpae et poenae, et pacem quantum ad consecutionem omnis boni; unde ter *agnus Dei*, dicitur. Praeparatio autem specialis sacerdotis sumentis fit per orationes quas privatim dicit, *Domine Jesu Christe*, et si quae aliae sunt.

whom this sacrament has its origin both as regards its substance — whence he says *creas* [you create] on account of the being of nature, *sanctificas* [you sanctify] on account of the being of the sacrament — and as regards its power — whence he says *vivificas* [you enliven] on account of the effect of grace, which is the life of the soul; *benedicis* [you bless] on account of the increase of grace; and as regards operation or use, whence he says *et praestas nobis* [you grant to us].

Oremus. Praeceptis salutaribus moniti, et divina institutione formati audemus dicere. Here is placed the reception of the sacrament, before which there is preparation both common and special. The common preparation is threefold: for first there is placed the petition of the sacrament in the Lord's Prayer, in which there is said, *Panem nostrum quotidianum da nobis hodie*; second the expiation of those receiving through the prayer of the priest: *Libera nos*; third the fulfillment of peace, at *Pax Domini*. For this sacrament is of sanctity and peace; and because the peace of Christ surpasses every sense, thus the petition of peace is begun by the priest, when he says, *Pax Domini*, and completed by the choir, when the *Agnus Dei* is said; and thus there is completed the three things begun by the priest, namely the *Gloria in excelsis*, which pertains to hope; the *Credo in unum Deum*, which pertains to faith; the *Pax Domini*, which pertains to charity. Yet the people asks for mercy as regards the removal of evil against the misery of fault and sin, and peace as regards the accomplishment of all good; whence the *Agnus Dei* is said three times. Yet the special preparation of the priest receiving is made through the prayers that he says privately, *Domine Jesu Christe*, and whatever others there are.

Tertia pars principalis est gratiarum actionis; et continet duo: rememorationem accepti beneficii in cantu antiphonae post communionem, et gratiarum actionem in oratione, quam sacerdos prosequitur, ut conformiter finis Missae principio respondeat.

Sciendum autem, quod in officio Missae, ubi passio repraesentatur, quaedam continentur verba Graeca, sicut, *kyrie eleison*, idest Domine miserere: quaedam Hebraica, sicut *alleluja*, idest laudate Deum; *Sabaoth*, idest exercituum; *hosanna*, salva obsecro; *amen*, idest vere, vel fiat: quaedam Latina, quae patent: quia his tribus linguis scriptus est titulus crucis Christi, Joan. 19.

The third principal part is that of thanksgiving; and it contains two things: the remembrance of the benefit received in the singing of the antiphon after communion, and the thanksgiving in prayer, which the priest proclaims, so that the end of the Mass might correspond to the beginning.

Yet it must be known that, in the office of the Mass, where the Passion is represented, there are contained certain Greek words, such as *Kyrie eleison*, i.e. "Lord, have mercy"; certain Hebrew words, such as *Alleluia*, i.e. "Praise God"; *Sabaoth*, i.e. "hosts"; *Hosanna*, "Save, I beg"; *Amen*, i.e. "Truly" or "Let it be done"; and certain Latin words, which are obvious — for the titulus of the cross of Christ was written in these three languages (John 19:20).

In IV Sent., D. 12, EX.

. . .[†] *In sacramento recordatio illius fit quod factum est semel.* Sacerdos enim non solum verbis, sed etiam factis, Christi passionem repraesentat.

Unde et in principio canonis tres cruces facit super illud: *haec dona, haec munera, haec sancta sacrificia illibata*, ad significandum trinam traditionem Christi, scilicet a Deo, Juda, et Judaeis. Secundo autem super illud: *benedictam, adscriptam, ratam* etc. facit tres communiter super utrumque, ad ostendendum quod tribus Christus est venditus, scilicet sacerdotibus, Scribis, et Pharisaeis. Duas autem facit divisim super corpus et sanguinem, ad ostendendum venditorem et venditum. Tertio facit duas super illud: *benedixit et fregit*: unam super corpus, aliam super sanguinem, ad ostendendum quod hoc sacramentum valet ad salutem corporis et animae. Et quia Dominus hoc sacramentum in mortis suae memoriam exercendum mandavit, ideo statim post consecrationem

---

† As in Distinction 8, so also here, St. Thomas had treated a few other things in this *expositio textus* before beginning his commentary on the actions of the Mass — namely what Christ looked like on the road to Emmaus, the heresy of Berengar of Tours, how Christ is absorbed by one who receives holy communion, the danger in store for a minister who deviates from the rite, and how to reconcile Christ's being put to death only once with his repeatedly offering himself to the Father at the Mass every day. Once again, despite the interest of those subjects, it seemed better to begin with the *expositio Missae* proper.

. . . "In the sacrament there is made the remembrance of what was done once." For the priest represents the Passion of Christ not only by words, but also by deeds.

Whence also at the beginning of the Canon, he makes three signs of the cross, at the words *haec dona, haec munera, haec sancta sacrificia illibata*, to signify the triple handing over of Christ, namely by God, by Judas, and by the Jews. Yet second, at the words *benedictam, adscriptam, ratam* etc., he makes three commonly over both, to show that Christ was sold to three, namely the priests, the scribes, and the Pharisees. Yet he makes two separately over the body and blood, to show the seller and the one sold. Third, he makes two at the words *benedixit et fregit*: one over the body, another over the blood, to show that this sacrament prevails for the health of body and of soul. And because the Lord commanded that this sacrament be carried out in memory of his death, thus immediately after the consecration, he represents the effigy of the cross by the extension of his arms. Whence also, as Innocent says, the words of consecration, which would have had to be placed at the end as the completion of the whole, are placed in the middle to observe the order of history; because the words of the Canon pertain principally to consecrating the Eucharist, but the signs to recalling the history. Fourth, he makes five signs of the cross at the words *hostiam puram* etc., to

brachiorum extensione crucis effigiem repraesentat. Unde etiam, ut Innocentius dicit, verba consecrationis, quae in fine ponenda essent quasi complementum totius, in medio ponuntur ad historiae ordinem observandum; quia verba canonis ad Eucharistiam consecrandam principaliter pertinent, sed signa ad historiam recolendam. Quarto facit quinque cruces super illud: *hostiam puram* etc. ad repraesentandum quinque plagas. Quinto facit duas super illud: *sacrosanctum filii tui corpus* etc. ad signandum vincula et flagella Christi. Et additur tertia, qua sacerdos seipsum signat super illud: *omni benedictione*; quia Christi vulnera, nostra sunt medicamenta. Vel per has tres cruces significatur triplex oratio, qua Christus orasse legitur Matth. 26, passione imminente. Sexto facit tres super illud: *sanctificas, vivificas, benedicis* etc. ad repraesentandum, quod Judaei ter dixerunt: *crucifige*, verbo crucifigentes Christum, quod fuit tertia hora. Septimo iterum facit tres super illud: *per ipsum, et in ipso, et cum ipso*, ad repraesentandum secundam crucifixionem, qua a militibus hora sexta post trium horarum spatium crucifixus est; vel ad repraesentandum tres ejus cruciatus, scilicet passionis, propassionis, compassionis. Deinde facit duas extra calicem super illud: *est tibi Deo patri omnipotenti in unitate Spiritus Sancti omnis honor et gloria*, ad repraesentandum separationem animae a corpore, quae facta est hora nona; vel propter sanguinem et aquam, quae de latere Christi profluxerunt.

Inclinationes etiam factae a sacerdote, signant Christi obedientiam ad patrem, ex qua mortem sustinuit.

Tacita etiam locutio exprimit consilium Judaeorum mortem Christi machinantium, vel discipulorum, qui palam Christum confiteri non audebant.

represent the five wounds. Fifth, he makes two at the words *sacrosanctum Filii tui corpus* etc., to signify the chains and scourgings of Christ. And a third is added, with which the priest signs himself at the words *omni benedictione*; because the wounds of Christ are our medicine. Or through these three crosses there is signified the threefold prayer by which Christ is read to have prayed in Matthew 26, when his Passion was imminent. Sixth, he makes three at the words *sanctificas, vivificas, benedicis* etc., to represent that the Jews said, *Crucify him*, three times, crucifying Christ by a word, which was at the third hour. Seventh, he again makes three at the words *Per ipsum, et in ipso, et cum ipso*, to represent the second crucifixion, by which he was crucified by the soldiers at the sixth hour after a span of three hours; or to represent his three tortures, namely of passion, of propassion, and of compassion. Then he makes two outside the chalice at the words *est tibi Deo Patri omnipotenti in unitate Spiritus Sancti omnis honor et gloria*, to represent the separation of soul from body, which was done at the ninth hour; or on account of the blood and water, which flowed forth from the side of Christ.

The bows made by the priest also signify Christ's obedience to the Father, out of which he endured death.

Also the silent speech expresses the counsel of the Jews plotting the death of Christ, or of the disciples, who were not bold to confess Christ openly.

Quid autem fractio significet, dictum est.

Quia autem commixtio corporis et sanguinis unionem
animae et corporis significat; ideo illa crucis signatio
quae fit super illa verba: *pax Domini sit semper vobiscum*,
magis pertinet ad resurrectionem, quae virtute Trinitatis
et tertia die facta est.

Quod autem quinquies se sacerdos ad populum convertit,
significat quod Dominus die resurrectionis quinquies
se manifestavit: primo Mariae Magdalenae, Joan. ult.
secundo Petro, Luc. ult. tertio mulieribus, Matth. ult.
quarto discipulis in Emaus, Lucae ultim. quinto discipulis in unum, Joan. ult.

Salutat autem populum septies ad septiformem gratiam
Spiritus Sancti ostendendam. *Sine quibus mortalis vita
duci non potest*; quia etsi possumus vitare singula, non
tamen omnia.

Yet what the Fraction signifies has been said (*In IV Sent.*, d. 12, q. 1, a. 3, qa. 3).

Yet because the mingling of the body and blood signifies the union of soul and body, thus that sign of the cross that is made over the words *Pax Domini sit semper vobiscum* rather pertains to the Resurrection, which was done by the power of the Trinity and on the third day.

Yet that the priest turns himself around to the people five times signifies that the Lord manifested himself on the day of the Resurrection five times: first to Mary Magdalene (John 20:14), second to Peter (Luke 24:34), third to the women (Matt 28:9), fourth to the disciples going to Emmaus (Luke 24:15), fifth to the disciples altogether (John 20:19).

Yet he greets the people seven times, to show the septiform grace of the Holy Spirit. "Without which mortal life cannot be led"; because although we can avoid each [sin], nevertheless not all.

Ad quartum sic proceditur. Videtur quod inconvenienter ordinentur ea quae circa hoc sacramentum dicuntur.

Hoc enim sacramentum verbis Christi consecratur, ut Ambrosius dicit, in libro de sacramentis. Non ergo debent aliqua alia in hoc sacramento dici quam verba Christi.

Praeterea, verba et facta Christi nobis per Evangelium innotescunt. Sed quaedam dicuntur circa consecrationem huius sacramenti quae in Evangeliis non ponuntur. Non enim legitur in Evangelio quod Christus in institutione huius sacramenti oculos ad caelum levaverit; similiter etiam in Evangeliis dicitur, accipite et comedite, nec ponitur omnes, cum in celebratione huius sacramenti dicatur, elevatis oculis in caelum, et iterum, accipite et manducate ex hoc omnes. Inconvenienter ergo huiusmodi verba dicuntur in celebratione huius sacramenti.

Praeterea, omnia alia sacramenta ordinantur ad salutem omnium fidelium. Sed in celebratione aliorum sacramentorum non fit communis oratio pro salute omnium fidelium et defunctorum. Ergo inconvenienter fit in hoc sacramento.

To the fourth it is proceeded thus. It seems that the things said around this sacrament are unfittingly ordered.

Objection 1. For this sacrament is consecrated by the words of Christ, as Ambrose says, in the book *De Sacramentis*. There should not be any other words said in this sacrament, therefore, besides the words of Christ.

Objection 2. Besides, the words and deeds of Christ are made known to us through the Gospel. But certain things are said around the consecration of this sacrament that are not found in the Gospels. For we do not read in the Gospel that Christ at the institution of this sacrament lifted his eyes to heaven; likewise also it says in the Gospels, *Accipite et comedite* [Take and eat], but *omnes* [all of you] is not found there, whereas in the celebration of this sacrament it is said, *elevatis oculis in caelum* [with eyes raised to heaven], and again, *Accipite et manducate ex hoc omnes* [Take and eat of this, all of you]. Unfittingly, therefore, are words of this kind said in the celebration of this sacrament.

Objection 3. Besides, all of the other sacraments are ordered to the salvation of all the faithful. But in the celebration of the other sacraments, no common prayer is made for the salvation of all the faithful and the departed. Unfittingly, therefore, is this done in this sacrament.

Praeterea, Baptismus dicitur specialiter fidei sacramentum. Ea ergo quae pertinent ad instructionem fidei, magis debent circa Baptismum tradi quam circa hoc sacramentum, sicut doctrina apostolica et evangelica.

Praeterea, in omni sacramento exigitur devotio fidelium. Non ergo magis in hoc sacramento quam in aliis deberet devotio fidelium excitari per laudes divinas et per admonitiones, puta cum dicitur, sursum corda.

Praeterea, minister huius sacramenti est sacerdos, ut dictum est. Omnia ergo quae in hoc sacramento dicuntur, a sacerdote dici deberent, et non quaedam a ministris, quaedam a choro.

Praeterea, hoc sacramentum per certitudinem operatur virtus divina. Superflue igitur sacerdos petit huius sacramenti perfectionem, cum dicit, *quam oblationem tu, Deus, in omnibus*, et cetera.

Praeterea, sacrificium novae legis multo est excellentius quam sacrificium antiquorum patrum. Inconvenienter ergo sacerdos petit quod hoc sacrificium habeatur sicut sacrificium Abel, Abrahae et Melchisedech.

Praeterea, corpus Christi, sicut non incoepit esse in hoc sacramento per loci mutationem, ut supra dictum est, ita etiam nec esse desinit. Inconvenienter ergo sacerdos petit, *iube haec perferri per manus sancti Angeli tui in sublime altare tuum.*

Objection 4. Besides, Baptism in particular is called the sacrament of faith. Those things, therefore, that pertain to the instruction of the faith, ought to be handed on in the context of Baptism rather than in the context of this sacrament, such as the apostolic and evangelical teaching.

Objection 5. Besides, in every sacrament the devotion of the faithful is necessary. No more in this sacrament than in the others, therefore, should the devotion of the faithful be aroused through divine praises and through admonitions, for example, where there is said, *Sursum corda*.

Objection 6. Besides, the minister of this sacrament is the priest, as has been said. Everything, therefore, that is said in this sacrament, ought to be said by the priest, and not certain things by the ministers, certain things by the choir.

Objection 7. Besides, divine power works this sacrament with certitude. Superfluously, therefore, does the priest ask for the perfection of this sacrament, when he says, *Quam oblationem tu, Deus, in omnibus*, etc.

Objection 8. Besides, the sacrifice of the new law is much more excellent than the sacrifice of the ancient fathers. Unfittingly, therefore, does the priest ask that this sacrifice be considered like the sacrifice of Abel, of Abraham, and of Melchizedek.

Objection 9. Besides, the body of Christ, as it did not begin to be in this sacrament through change of place, as has been said (*ST* IIIa, Q. 75, a. 2, c.), so neither does it cease to be. Unfittingly, therefore, does the priest ask, *Iube haec perferri per manus sancti Angeli tui in sublime altare tuum*.

Sed contra est quod dicitur de Consecr., dist. I, *Iacobus frater domini secundum carnem, et Basilius Caesariensis episcopus, ediderunt Missae celebrationem*. Ex quorum auctoritate patet convenienter singula circa hoc dici.

Respondeo dicendum quod, quia in hoc sacramento totum mysterium nostrae salutis comprehenditur, ideo prae ceteris sacramentis cum maiori solemnitate agitur. Et quia scriptum est Eccle. IV, *custodi pedem tuum ingrediens domum domini*, et Eccli. XVIII, *ante orationem praepara animam tuam*, ideo ante celebrationem huius mysterii, primo quidem praemittitur praeparatio quaedam ad digne agenda ea quae sequuntur. Cuius praeparationis prima pars est laus divina, quae fit in introitu, secundum illud Psalmi, *sacrificium laudis honorificabit me, et illic iter quo ostendam illi salutare Dei*. Et sumitur hoc, ut pluries, de Psalmis, vel saltem cum Psalmo cantatur, quia, ut Dionysius dicit, in III cap. Eccles. Hier., Psalmi comprehendunt per modum laudis quidquid in sacra Scriptura continetur.

Secunda pars continet commemorationem praesentis miseriae, dum misericordia petitur, dicendo kyrie eleison ter pro persona patris; ter pro persona filii, cum dicitur Christe eleison; et ter pro persona spiritus sancti, cum subditur kyrie eleison; contra triplicem miseriam ignorantiae, culpae et poenae; vel ad significandum quod omnes personae sunt in se invicem.

But to the contrary is what is said in *De Consecratione*, Distinction 1: *James the brother of the Lord according to the flesh, and Basil the bishop of Caesarea, taught the celebration of the Mass*. From whose authority it is clear that each thing said around this is said fittingly.

I answer that it must be said that, because in this sacrament the whole mystery of our salvation is embraced, thus it is carried out with greater solemnity than the other sacraments. And because it is written, *Guard your foot entering the house of the Lord* (Eccl 4:17), and, *Before prayer, prepare your soul* (Sir 18:23), thus before the celebration of this mystery, first of all there is a certain preparation for carrying out worthily the things that follow. The first part of this preparation is the divine praise, which is done in the Introit, according to Psalm 49:23, *A sacrifice of praise shall honor me, and there is the way by which I shall show him the salvation of God*. And this is usually taken from the Psalms, or at least it is sung with a Psalm, because, as Denys said in Chapter 3 of the *Ecclesiastical Hierarchy*, "The Psalms embrace through the mode of praise whatever is contained in sacred scripture."

The second part contains the commemoration of present misery, while mercy is begged, saying *Kyrie eleison* three times for the person of the Father; three times for the person of the Son, when *Christe eleison* is said; and three times for the person of the Holy Spirit, when *Kyrie eleison* is added; against the threefold misery of ignorance, fault, and punishment; or to signify that all three persons are in one another.

Tertia autem pars commemorat caelestem gloriam, ad quam tendimus post praesentem miseriam, dicendo, gloria in excelsis Deo. Quae cantatur in festis, in quibus commemoratur caelestis gloria, intermittitur autem in officiis luctuosis, quae ad commemorationem miseriae pertinent.

Quarta autem pars continet orationem, quam sacerdos pro populo facit, ut digni habeantur tantis mysteriis.

Secundo autem praemittitur instructio fidelis populi, quia hoc sacramentum est mysterium fidei, ut supra habitum est. Quae quidem instructio dispositive quidem fit per doctrinam prophetarum et apostolorum, quae in Ecclesia legitur per lectores et subdiaconos. Post quam lectionem, cantatur a choro graduale, quod significat profectum vitae; et alleluia, quod significat spiritualem exultationem; vel tractus, in officiis luctuosis, qui significat spiritualem gemitum. Haec enim consequi debent in populo ex praedicta doctrina. Perfecte autem populus instruitur per doctrinam Christi in Evangelio contentam, quae a summis ministris legitur, scilicet a diaconibus. Et quia Christo credimus tanquam divinae veritati, secundum illud Ioan. VIII, *si veritatem dico vobis, quare vos non creditis mihi?*, Lecto Evangelio, symbolum fidei cantatur, in quo populus ostendit se per fidem doctrinae Christi assentire. Cantatur autem hoc symbolum in festis de quibus fit aliqua mentio in hoc symbolo, sicut in festis Christi et beatae virginis, et apostolorum, qui hanc fidem fundaverunt, et in aliis huiusmodi.

Yet the third part commemorates heavenly glory, to which we tend after the present misery, saying, *Gloria in excelsis Deo*. Which is sung on feasts, in which heavenly glory is commemorated, yet is omitted in offices of mourning, which pertain to the commemoration of misery.

Yet the fourth part contains the oration, which the priest makes for the people, so that they might be considered worthy of such great mysteries.

Yet second there is the Instruction of the faithful people, because this sacrament is a mystery of faith, as has been said above. Which Instruction indeed is done dispositively through the doctrine of the prophets and apostles, which is read in the Church by lectors and subdeacons. After which reading, the Gradual is sung by the choir, which signifies progress of life; and the Alleluia, which signifies spiritual exultation; or the Tract, in mournful offices, which signifies spiritual groaning. For these things ought to be in the people from the aforementioned doctrine. Yet the people is perfectly instructed through the doctrine of Christ contained in the Gospel, which is read by the highest ministers, namely by the deacons. And because we believe Christ as divine truth, according to John 8:46, *If I speak the truth to you, why do you not believe me?*, with the Gospel having been read, the Symbol of the faith is sung, in which the people show that they assent through faith to the doctrine of Christ. Yet this Symbol is sung on feasts about which some mention is made in this Symbol, as on feasts of Christ and of the Blessed Virgin, and of the Apostles, who founded this faith, and on others of this sort.

Sic igitur populo praeparato et instructo, acceditur ad celebrationem mysterii. Quod quidem et offertur ut sacrificium, et consecratur et sumitur ut sacramentum, primo enim peragitur oblatio; secundo, consecratio materiae oblatae; tertio, perceptio eiusdem.

Circa oblationem vero duo aguntur, scilicet laus populi, in cantu offertorii, per quod significatur laetitia offerentium; et oratio sacerdotis, qui petit ut oblatio populi sit Deo accepta. Unde, I Paralip., dixit David, *ego in simplicitate cordis mei obtuli universa haec, et populum tuum qui hic repertus est, vidi cum ingenti gaudio tibi offerre donaria*, et postea orat, dicens, *domine Deus, custodi hanc voluntatem.*

Deinde, circa consecrationem, quae supernaturali virtute agitur, primo excitatur populus ad devotionem in praefatione, unde et monetur sursum corda habere ad dominum. Et ideo, finita praefatione, populus cum devotione laudat divinitatem Christi cum Angelis, dicens, sanctus, sanctus, sanctus; et humanitatem cum pueris, dicens, benedictus qui venit. Deinde sacerdos secreto commemorat, primo quidem, illos pro quibus hoc sacrificium offertur, scilicet pro universali Ecclesia, et pro his qui in sublimitate sunt constituti, I Tim. II; et specialiter quosdam qui offerunt vel pro quibus offertur. Secundo, commemorat sanctos, quorum patrocinia implorat pro praedictis, cum dicit, communicantes et memoriam venerantes, et cetera. Tertio, petitionem concludit, cum dicit, hanc igitur oblationem etc. ut fiat oblatio pro quibus offertur salutaris.

Therefore, with the people thus prepared and instructed, it continues to the celebration of the mystery. Which indeed is both offered as a sacrifice, and consecrated and received as a sacrament, for first the Oblation is performed; second, the consecration of the matter offered; third, the reception of the same.

Whereas around the Oblation two things are carried out, namely the praise of the people, in the chant of the Offertory, through which the happiness of those offering is signified; and the prayer of the priest, which asks that the oblation of the people may be acceptable to God. Whence David said, in 1 Chronicles 29:17, *In the simplicity of my heart I have offered all these things, and I have seen with great joy your people who are found here to offer you gifts*, and afterward he prays, saying, *Lord God, regard this will* (1 Chr 29:18).

Then, around the consecration, which is carried out by supernatural power, first the people are excited to devotion in the Preface, whence also they are commanded to have their hearts up [*Sursum corda*] toward the Lord. And thus, with the Preface finished, with devotion the people praises the divinity of Christ with the angels, saying, *Sanctus, Sanctus, Sanctus*; and his humanity with the children, saying, *Benedictus qui venit*. Then the priest secretly commemorates, first of all, those for whom this sacrifice is offered, namely for the universal Church, and for those who are set in high places (1 Tim 2:2); and specifically certain ones who offer or for whom it is offered. Second, he commemorates the saints, whose patronage he implores for those mentioned above, when he says, *Communicantes et memoriam venerantes* etc. Third, he concludes the petition, when he says, *Hanc igitur*

Deinde accedit ad ipsam consecrationem. In qua primo petit consecrationis effectum, cum dicit, quam oblationem tu Deus. Secundo, consecrationem peragit per verba salvatoris, cum dicit, qui pridie, et cetera. Tertio, excusat praesumptionem per obedientiam ad mandatum Christi, cum dicit, unde et memores. Quarto, petit hoc sacrificium peractum esse Deo acceptum, cum dicit, supra quae propitio, et cetera. Quinto, petit huius sacrificii et sacramenti effectum, primo quidem, quantum ad ipsos sumentes, cum dicit, supplices te rogamus; secundo, quantum ad mortuos, qui iam sumere non possunt, cum dicit, memento etiam, domine, etc.; tertio, specialiter quantum ad ipsos sacerdotes offerentes, cum dicit, nobis quoque peccatoribus et cetera.

Deinde agitur de perceptione sacramenti. Et primo quidem, praeparatur populus ad percipiendum. Primo quidem, per orationem communem totius populi, quae est oratio dominica, in qua petimus panem nostrum quotidianum nobis dari; et etiam privatam, quam specialiter sacerdos pro populo offert, cum dicit, libera nos, quaesumus, domine. Secundo, praeparatur populus per pacem, quae datur dicendo, agnus Dei, est enim hoc sacramentum unitatis et pacis, ut supra dictum est. In Missis autem defunctorum, in quibus hoc sacrificium offertur non pro pace praesenti, sed pro requie mortuorum, pax intermittitur.

Deinde sequitur perceptio sacramenti, primo percipiente sacerdote, et postmodum aliis dante; quia, ut dicit

oblationem etc., so that the oblation might be made salvific for whom it is offered.

Then he comes to the consecration itself. In which first he asks for the effect of the consecration, when he says, *Quam oblationem tu Deus*. Second, he performs the consecration through the words of the Savior, when he says, *Qui pridie* etc. Third, he excuses himself of presumption through obedience to the mandate of Christ, when he says, *Unde et memores*. Fourth, he asks that this sacrifice, having been completed, may be acceptable to God, when he says, *Supra quae propitio* etc. Fifth, he asks for the effect of this sacrifice and sacrament, first of all, as regards those receiving, when he says, *Supplices te rogamus*; second, as regards the dead, who can no longer receive, when he says, *Memento etiam, Domine* etc.; third, specifically as regards those priests offering, when he says, *Nobis quoque peccatoribus* etc.

Then the reception of the sacrament is carried out. And first of all, the people are prepared to receive. First indeed, through the common prayer of the whole people, which is the Lord's Prayer, in which we ask that our daily bread should be given to us; and also through private prayer, which the priest specifically offers for the people, when he says, *Libera nos, quaesumus, Domine*. Second, the people are prepared through peace, which is given by saying, *Agnus Dei*, for this is the sacrament of unity and peace, as was said above. Yet in Masses for the dead, in which this sacrifice is offered not for present peace, but for the rest of the dead, the Pax is omitted.

Then there follows the reception of the sacrament, first with the priest receiving, and afterward with him giving

Dionysius, III cap. Eccles. Hier., qui aliis divina tradit, primo debet ipse particeps esse.

Ultimo autem tota Missae celebratio in gratiarum actione terminatur, populo exultante pro sumptione mysterii, quod significat cantus post communionem; et sacerdote per orationem gratias offerente, sicut et Christus, celebrata cena cum discipulis, hymnum dixit, ut dicitur Matth. XXVI.

Ad primum ergo dicendum quod consecratio solis verbis Christi conficitur. Alia vero necesse fuit addere ad praeparationem populi sumentis, ut dictum est.

Ad secundum dicendum quod, sicut dicitur Ioan. ult., multa sunt a domino facta vel dicta quae Evangelistae non scripserunt. Inter quae fuit hoc quod dominus oculos levavit in caelum in cena, quod tamen Ecclesia ex traditione apostolorum habuit. Rationabile enim videtur ut qui in suscitatione Lazari, ut habetur Ioan. XI, et in oratione quam pro discipulis fecit, Ioan. XVII, oculos levavit ad patrem, in huius sacramenti institutione multo magis hoc fecerit, tanquam in re potiori.

Quod autem dicitur manducate, et non comedite, non differt quantum ad sensum. Nec multum refert quid dicatur, praesertim cum verba illa non sint de forma, ut supra dictum est.

to the others, as Denys says in Chapter 3 of the *Ecclesiastical Hierarchy*, "He who hands on divine things to others, ought first to be a partaker himself."

Yet last the whole celebration of the Mass is terminated in thanksgiving, with the people rejoicing for the reception of the mystery, which the chant after communion signifies; and with the priest offering thanks through the oration, just as Christ likewise, when he had celebrated the supper with his disciples, said a hymn, as is said in Matthew 26:30.

To the first, therefore, it must be said that the consecration is confected by the words of Christ alone. Whereas other things were necessary to add for the preparation of the people receiving, as has been said.

To the second, therefore, it must be said that, just as it is said in John 21:15, many things were done or said by the Lord that the Evangelists did not write down. Among which was that the Lord raised his eyes to heaven at the supper, which nevertheless the Church has from the tradition of the apostles. For it seems reasonable that he who raised his eyes to the Father at the raising of Lazarus, in John 11:41, and in the prayer that he made for his disciples, in John 17:1, much more would do so at the institution of this sacrament, since this is more powerful.

Yet that *manducate* [eat] is said, and not *comedite* [eat], does not differ as regards the meaning. Nor does it matter much what is said, especially since those words are not a part of the form, as was said above.

Quod autem additur omnes, intelligitur in verbis Evangelii, licet non exprimatur, quia ipse dixerat, Ioan. VI, *nisi manducaveritis carnem filii hominis, non habebitis vitam in vobis.*

Ad tertium dicendum quod Eucharistia est sacramentum totius ecclesiasticae unitatis. Et ideo specialiter in hoc sacramento, magis quam in aliis, debet fieri mentio de omnibus quae pertinent ad salutem totius Ecclesiae.

Ad quartum dicendum quod duplex est instructio. Una, quae fit noviter imbuendis, scilicet catechumenis. Et talis instructio fit circa Baptismum. Alia autem est instructio in qua instruitur fidelis populus, qui communicat huic mysterio. Et talis instructio fit in hoc sacramento. Et tamen ab hac instructione non repelluntur etiam catechumeni et infideles. Unde dicitur de Consecr., dist. I, *episcopus nullum prohibeat Ecclesiam ingredi et audire verbum Dei, sive gentilem sive haereticum sive Iudaeum, usque ad Missam catechumenorum,* in qua scilicet continetur instructio fidei.

Ad quintum dicendum quod in hoc sacramento maior devotio requiritur quam in aliis sacramentis, propter hoc quod in hoc sacramento totus Christus continetur. Et etiam communior, quia in hoc sacramento requiritur devotio totius populi, pro quo sacrificium offertur, et non solum percipientium sacramentum, sicut in aliis sacramentis. Et ideo, sicut Cyprianus dicit, *sacerdos,*

Yet that *omnes* [all of you] is added is understood in the words of the Gospel, although granted it is not expressed, because he had said, in John 6:54, *Unless you should eat the flesh of the Son of Man, you shall not have life in you*.

To the third it must be said that the Eucharist is the sacrament of the unity of the whole Church. And thus particularly in this sacrament, more than in the others, mention ought to be made of everything that pertains to the salvation of the whole Church.

To the fourth it must be said that instruction is twofold. One, which is made for those newly initiated, namely for catechumens. And such an instruction is made in the context of Baptism. Yet the other is the instruction in which the faithful people is instructed, who communicate in this mystery. And such an instruction is made in this sacrament. And nevertheless even catechumens and infidels are not driven away from this instruction. Whence it is said in *De Consecratione*, Distinction 1, "Let the bishop prohibit no one from entering the Church and hearing the word of God, whether gentile or heretic or Jew, all the way through the Mass of the catechumens," namely in which the instruction of the faith in contained.

To the fifth it must be said that greater devotion is required in this sacrament than in the other sacraments, on account of the fact that the whole Christ is contained in this sacrament. And also more common devotion is required, because in this sacrament there is required the devotion of the whole people, for whom the sacrifice is offered, and not only of those receiving the sacrament,

praefatione praemissa, parat fratrum mentes, dicendo, sur-
sum corda, ut, dum respondet plebs, habemus ad dominum,
admoneatur nihil aliud se cogitare quam Deum.

Ad sextum dicendum quod in hoc sacramento, sicut dictum est, tanguntur ea quae pertinent ad totam Ecclesiam.
Et ideo quaedam dicuntur a choro, quae pertinent ad
populum. Quorum quaedam chorus totaliter prosequitur,
quae scilicet toti populo inspirantur. Quaedam vero
populus prosequitur, sacerdote inchoante, qui personam
Dei gerit, in signum quod talia pervenerunt ad populum ex revelatione divina, sicut fides et gloria caelestis.
Et ideo sacerdos inchoat symbolum fidei et gloria in
excelsis Deo. Quaedam vero dicuntur per ministros,
sicut doctrina novi et veteris testamenti, in signum quod
per ministros a Deo missos est haec doctrina populis
nuntiata. Quaedam vero sacerdos solus prosequitur, quae
scilicet ad proprium officium sacerdotis pertinent, ut
scilicet dona et preces offerat pro populo, sicut dicitur
Heb. V. In his tamen quaedam dicit publice, quae scilicet
pertinent et ad sacerdotem et ad populum, sicut sunt
orationes communes. Quaedam vero pertinent ad solum
sacerdotem, sicut oblatio et consecratio. Et ideo quae
circa haec sunt dicenda occulte a sacerdote dicuntur.
In utrisque tamen excitat attentionem populi, dicendo,
dominus vobiscum; et expectat assensum dicentium,
amen. Et ideo in his quae secreto dicuntur, publice
praemittit, dominus vobiscum, et subiungit, per omnia
saecula saeculorum. Vel secrete aliqua sacerdos dicit in
signum quod, circa Christi passionem, discipuli non
nisi occulte Christum confitebantur.

as in the other sacraments. And thus, as Cyprian says, "The priest, just before the Preface, prepares the minds of the brethren, saying, *Sursum corda*, so that, while the people responds, *Habemus ad Dominum*, they might be admonished to think of nothing other than God."

To the sixth it must be said that in this sacrament, as has been said, things that pertain to the whole Church are mentioned. And thus certain things are said by the choir, which pertain to the people. Some of which the choir pronounces in their entirety, namely those that are inspired for the whole people. Whereas others the people pronounce after they have been intoned by the priest, who bears the person of God, as a sign that such things come to the people from divine revelation, such as faith and heavenly glory. And thus the priest intones the Symbol of faith and the *Gloria in Excelsis Deo*. Whereas some are said through the ministers, such as the doctrine of the New and Old Testaments, as a sign that this doctrine was announced to the people through ministers sent by God. Whereas some are pronounced by the priest alone, namely those that pertain to the proper office of the priest, namely to offer gifts and prayers for the people, as is said in Hebrews 5:1. Among these, nevertheless, some are said publicly, namely those that pertain both to the priest and to the people, like the common orations. Whereas some pertain to the priest alone, like the oblation and the consecration. And thus the things to be said around these are said secretly by the priest. Nevertheless, in both kinds he excites the attention of the people, saying, *Dominus vobiscum*; and he awaits their assent when they say, *Amen*. And thus in those things that are said secretly, he first says publicly, *Dominus vobiscum*, and he adds, *per omnia saecula*

Ad septimum dicendum quod efficacia verborum sacramentalium impediri potest per intentionem sacerdotis. Nec tamen est inconveniens quod a Deo petamus id quod certissime scimus ipsum facturum, sicut Christus, Ioan. XVII, petiit suam clarificationem.

Non tamen ibi videtur sacerdos orare ut consecratio impleatur, sed ut nobis fiat fructuosa, unde signanter dicit, ut nobis corpus et sanguis fiat. Et hoc significant verba quae praemittit dicens, hanc oblationem facere digneris benedictam, secundum Augustinum, idest, per quam benedicimur, scilicet per gratiam; adscriptam, idest, per quam in caelo adscribimur; ratam, idest, per quam visceribus Christi censeamur; rationabilem, idest, per quam a bestiali sensu exuamur; acceptabilem, idest, ut, qui nobis ipsis displicemus, per hanc acceptabiles eius unico filio simus.

Ad octavum dicendum quod, licet hoc sacrificium ex seipso praeferatur omnibus antiquis sacrificiis, tamen sacrificia antiquorum fuerunt Deo acceptissima ex eorum devotione. Petit ergo sacerdos ut hoc sacrificium acceptetur Deo ex devotione offerentium, sicut illa accepta fuerunt Deo.

saeculorum. Or else the priest says some things secretly as a sign that, around the time of Christ's Passion, the disciples confessed Christ only secretly.

To the seventh it must be said that the efficacy of the sacramental words can be impeded through the intention of the priest. And regardless, it is not unfitting that we should ask of God what we know is most certainly going to be done, like Christ, in John 17:1–5, asked for his glorification.

Nevertheless the priest does not seem to be praying there that the consecration may be fulfilled, but rather that it may be fruitful for us, whence he says significantly, *ut nobis corpus et sanguis fiat* [that it may be made the body and blood for us]. And the words that he says beforehand signify this: *hanc oblationem facere digneris benedictam* — according to Augustine, that is, through which we are blessed, namely through grace; *adscriptam* — that is, through which we are inscribed in heaven; *ratam* — that is, through which we may be counted among the parts of Christ's body; *rationabilem* — that is, through which we are stripped of bestial sense; *acceptabilem* — that is, that we who displease even ourselves, through this may be acceptable to his only Son.

To the eighth it must be said that, although this sacrifice of itself is preferred to all the ancient sacrifices, nevertheless the sacrifices of the ancients were most acceptable to God from their devotion. The priest, therefore, asks that this sacrifice might be accepted by God from the devotion of those offering, just as those had been accepted by God.

Ad nonum dicendum quod sacerdos non petit quod species sacramentales deferantur in caelum; neque corpus Christi verum, quod ibi esse non desinit. Sed petit hoc pro corpore mystico, quod scilicet in hoc sacramento significatur, ut scilicet orationes et populi et sacerdotis Angelus assistens divinis mysteriis Deo repraesentet; secundum illud Apoc. VIII, *ascendit fumus incensorum de oblationibus sanctorum de manu Angeli*. Sublime autem altare Dei dicitur vel ipsa Ecclesia triumphans, in quam transferri petimus, vel ipse Deus, cuius participationem petimus; de hoc enim altari dicitur Exod. XX, *non ascendes ad altare meum per gradus, idest, in Trinitate gradus non facies*. Vel per Angelum intelligitur ipse Christus, qui est magni consilii Angelus, qui corpus suum mysticum Deo patri coniungit et Ecclesiae triumphanti.

Et propter hoc etiam Missa nominatur. Quia per Angelum sacerdos preces ad Deum mittit, sicut populus per sacerdotem. Vel quia Christus est hostia nobis missa. Unde et in fine Missae diaconus in festis diebus populum licentiat, dicens, *ite, Missa est*, scilicet hostia ad Deum per Angelum, ut scilicet sit Deo accepta.

To the ninth it must be said that the priest does not ask that the sacramental species should be taken into heaven; nor the true body of Christ, which never ceased to be there. But he asks this for the mystical body, namely that which is signified in this sacrament, namely that the angel assisting at the divine mysteries might present the prayers of the people and the priest before God; according to Revelation 8:4: *The smoke of incense rose from the offerings of the holy ones from the hand of the angel*. Yet the *sublime altare* [lofty altar] of God refers either to the Church triumphant, into which we ask to be transferred, or else to God himself, since we are asking to participate in him; for the altar refers to this in Exodus 20:26: *Not ascending to my altar through grades* — that is, you shall not make grades in the Trinity. Or else through the angel is understood Christ himself, who is the Angel of great counsel, who joins his mystical body to God the Father and to the Church triumphant.

And it is on account of this that the Mass is named. For the priest sends prayers to God through the angel, as the people do through the priest. Or because Christ is sent to us as a host. Whence also at the end of the Mass the deacon on feast days dismisses the people, saying, *Ite missa est* — namely, the host is sent to God through the angel, namely so that it might be acceptable to God.

Ad quintum sic proceditur. Videtur quod ea quae in celebratione huius sacramenti aguntur, non sunt convenientia.

Hoc enim sacramentum ad novum testamentum pertinet, ut ex forma ipsius apparet. In novo autem testamento non sunt observandae caeremoniae veteris testamenti. Ad quas pertinebat quod sacerdos et ministri aqua lavabantur quando accedebant ad offerendum, legitur enim Exod. XXX, *lavabunt Aaron et filii eius manus suas ac pedes quando ingressuri sunt ad altare*. Non est ergo conveniens quod sacerdos lavet manus suas inter Missarum solemnia.

Praeterea, ibidem dominus mandavit quod sacerdos adoleret incensum suave fragrans super altare quod erat ante propitiatorium. Quod etiam pertinebat ad caeremoniam veteris testamenti. Inconvenienter ergo sacerdos in Missa thurificatione utitur.

Praeterea, ea quae in sacramentis Ecclesiae aguntur, non sunt iteranda. Inconvenienter ergo sacerdos iterat crucesignationes super hoc sacramentum.

To the fifth it is proceeded thus. It seems that the things done in celebration of this sacrament are not fitting.

Objection 1. For this sacrament pertains to the New Testament, as is clear from its form. Yet in the New Testament, the ceremonies of the Old Testament are not to be observed. To which it pertained that the priest and the ministers would wash with water when they were going to make offerings, for we read in Exodus 30:19–20, *Aaron and his sons shall wash their hands and feet when they are to enter unto the altar*. It is not fitting, therefore, that the priest should wash his hands among the solemnities of the Mass.

Objection 2. Besides, in the same place, the Lord commanded that the priest should burn sweet-smelling incense upon the altar that was before the propitiatory. Which also pertained to the ceremony of the Old Testament. Unfittingly, therefore, does the priest use incensation in the Mass.

Objection 3. Besides, those things that are done in the sacraments of the Church must not be repeated. Unfittingly, therefore, does the priest repeat the signs of the cross over this sacrament.

Praeterea, apostolus dicit, Heb. VII, *sine ulla contradictione, quod minus est a maiori benedicitur*. Sed Christus, qui est in hoc sacramento post consecrationem, est multo maior sacerdote. Inconvenienter igitur sacerdos post consecrationem benedicit hoc sacramentum cruce signando.

Praeterea, in sacramento Ecclesiae nihil debet fieri quod ridiculosum videatur. Videtur autem ridiculosum gesticulationes facere, ad quas pertinere videtur quod sacerdos quandoque brachia extendit, manus iungit, digitos complicat, et seipsum incurvat. Ergo hoc non debet fieri in hoc sacramento.

Praeterea, ridiculosum etiam videtur quod sacerdos multoties se ad populum vertit, multoties etiam populum salutat. Non ergo debent haec fieri in celebratione huius sacramenti.

Praeterea, apostolus, I Cor. I, pro inconvenienti habet quod Christus sit divisus. Sed post consecrationem Christus est in hoc sacramento. Inconvenienter igitur hostia frangitur a sacerdote.

Praeterea, ea quae in hoc sacramento aguntur, passionem Christi repraesentant. Sed in passione Christi corpus fuit divisum in locis quinque vulnerum. Ergo corpus Christi in quinque partes frangi debet, magis quam in tres.

Praeterea, totum corpus Christi in hoc sacramento seorsum consecratur a sanguine. Inconvenienter igitur una pars eius sanguini miscetur.

Objection 4. Besides, the Apostle says, *Without any contradiction, the lesser is blessed by the greater* (Heb 7:7). But Christ, who is in this sacrament after the consecration, is much greater than the priest. Unfittingly, therefore, does the priest bless this sacrament after the consecration by making the sign of the cross.

Objection 5. Besides, in a sacrament of the Church nothing ought to be done that seems ridiculous. Yet it seems ridiculous to make gesticulations, which it would seem that the priest does when at various times he extends his arms, joins his hands, pinches his fingers, and bows down. Therefore, this should not be done in this sacrament.

Objection 6. Besides, it also seems ridiculous that the priest turns around to the people repeatedly, that he greets the people repeatedly. Therefore, these things should not be done in the celebration of this sacrament.

Objection 7. Besides, the Apostle, in 1 Corinthians 13, deems it unfitting that Christ should be divided. But after the consecration, Christ is in this sacrament. Unfittingly, therefore, is the host broken by the priest.

Objection 8. Besides, the things done in this sacrament represent the Passion of Christ. But in the Passion, the body of Christ was divided at the sites of the five wounds. Therefore, the body of Christ ought to be broken into five parts, rather than three.

Objection 9. Besides, the whole body of Christ in this sacrament is consecrated apart from the blood. Unfittingly, therefore, is one part of it mixed into the blood.

Praeterea, sicut corpus Christi proponitur in hoc sacramento ut cibus, ita et sanguis Christi ut potus. Sed
sumptioni corporis Christi non adiungitur in celebratione Missae alius corporalis cibus. Inconvenienter igitur
sacerdos, post sumptionem sanguinis Christi, vinum
non consecratum sumit.

Praeterea, veritas debet respondere figurae. Sed de agno
paschali, qui fuit figura huius sacramenti, mandatur
quod *non remaneret ex eo quidquam usque mane*. Inconvenienter ergo hostiae consecratae reservantur, et non
statim sumuntur.

Praeterea, sacerdos pluraliter loquitur audientibus, puta
cum dicit, dominus vobiscum, et, gratias agamus. Sed
inconveniens videtur pluraliter loqui uni soli, et maxime
minori. Ergo inconveniens videtur quod sacerdos, uno
tantum ministro praesente, celebret Missam. Sic igitur
videtur quod inconvenienter aliqua agantur in celebratione huius sacramenti.

Sed in contrarium est Ecclesiae consuetudo, quae errare
non potest, utpote spiritu sancto instructa.

Respondeo dicendum quod, sicut supra dictum est,
in sacramentis aliquid dupliciter significatur, scilicet
verbis et factis, ad hoc quod sit perfectior significatio.
Significantur autem verbis in celebratione huius sacramenti quaedam pertinentia ad passionem Christi, quae
repraesentatur in hoc sacramento; vel etiam ad corpus
mysticum, quod significatur in hoc sacramento; et quaedam pertinentia ad usum sacramenti, qui debet esse

Objection 10. Besides, just as the body of Christ is put forth in this sacrament as food, so also the blood of Christ as drink. But in the celebration of the Mass, no other bodily food is added to the consumption of the body of Christ. Unfittingly, therefore, does the priest, after consuming the blood of Christ, consume unconsecrated wine.

Objection 11. Besides, the truth ought to correspond to the figure. But concerning the paschal lamb, which was a figure of this sacrament, it was commanded that *nothing of it would remain until morning* (Ex 12:10). Unfittingly, therefore, are consecrated hosts reserved, and not consumed at once.

Objection 12. Besides, the priest speaks plurally to the listeners, for example when he says, *Dominus vobiscum*, and *Gratias agamus*. But it seems unfitting for him to speak plurally to just one person, and especially to an inferior. Therefore, it seems unfitting that the priest, with just one server present, should celebrate the Mass. And thus it seems that some things are done unfittingly in the celebration of this sacrament.

But to the contrary is the custom of the Church, who cannot err, as she is instructed by the Holy Spirit.

I answer that it must be said that, as has been said above, in the sacraments something is signified in a twofold way, namely by words and by deeds, so that the signification might be more perfect. Yet in the celebration of this sacrament, there are signified through words certain things pertaining to the Passion of Christ, which is represented in this sacrament; or also to the mystical body, which is signified in this sacrament; and certain things pertaining

cum devotione et reverentia. Et ideo in celebratione huius mysterii quaedam aguntur ad repraesentandum passionem Christi; vel etiam dispositionem corporis mystici; et quaedam aguntur pertinentia ad devotionem et reverentiam usus huius sacramenti.

Ad primum ergo dicendum quod ablutio manuum fit in celebratione Missae propter reverentiam huius sacramenti. Et hoc dupliciter. Primo quidem, quia aliqua pretiosa tractare non consuevimus nisi manibus ablutis. Unde indecens videtur quod ad tantum sacramentum aliquis accedat manibus, etiam corporaliter, inquinatis. Secundo, propter significationem. Quia, ut Dionysius dicit, III cap. Eccles. Hier., extremitatum ablutio significat emundationem etiam a minimis peccatis, secundum illud Ioan. XIII, *qui lotus est, non indiget nisi ut pedes lavet.* Et talis emundatio requiritur ab eo qui accedit ad hoc sacramentum. Quod etiam significatur per confessionem quae fit ante introitum Missae. Et hoc idem significabat ablutio sacerdotum in veteri lege, ut ibidem Dionysius dicit. Nec tamen Ecclesia hoc servat tanquam caeremoniale veteris legis praeceptum, sed quasi ab Ecclesia institutum, sicut quiddam secundum se conveniens. Et ideo non eodem modo observatur sicut tunc. Praetermittitur enim pedum ablutio, et servatur ablutio manuum, quae potest fieri magis in promptu, et quae sufficit ad significandam perfectam munditiam. Cum enim manus sit organum organorum, ut dicitur in III de anima, omnia opera attribuuntur manibus. Unde et in Psalmo dicitur, *lavabo inter innocentes manus meas.*

to the use of the sacrament, which ought to be with devotion and reverence. And thus in the celebration of this mystery, certain things are done to represent the Passion of Christ; or also the disposition of the mystical body; and certain things are done pertaining to the devotion and reverence of the use of this sacrament.

To the first, therefore, it must be said that the washing of the hands is done in the celebration of the Mass out of reverence for this sacrament. And this in two ways. First of all, because we are not accustomed to handling any precious things unless our hands have been cleansed. Whence it seems indecent that anyone should approach so great a sacrament with hands that are, even bodily, unwashed. Second, on account of its signification. Because, as Denys says in Chapter 3 of the *Ecclesiastical Hierarchy*, the washing of the extremities signifies the cleansing from even the smallest of sins, according to John 13:10: *He who has been bathed does not need anything but to wash his feet*. And such cleansing is required of him who approaches this sacrament. Which also is signified through the confession that is made before the Introit of the Mass. And the washing of the priests in the Old Law signified this same thing, as Denys says in the same place. Nor nevertheless does the Church observe this as a ceremonial precept of the Old Law, but rather as instituted by the Church, as something fitting in itself. And thus it is not observed in the same way now as then. For the washing of the feet is omitted, and the washing of the hands is preserved, which can be done more readily, and this suffices to signify perfect cleansing. For since the hand is the organ of organs, as is said in Book 3 of the *De Anima*, all works are attributed to the hands. Whence also in Psalm 25:6 it is said, *I shall wash my hands among the innocent*.

Ad secundum dicendum quod thurificatione non utimur quasi caeremoniali praecepto legis, sed sicut Ecclesiae statuto. Unde non eodem modo utimur sicut in veteri lege erat statutum. Pertinet autem ad duo. Primo quidem, ad reverentiam huius sacramenti, ut scilicet per bonum odorem depellatur si quid corporaliter pravi odoris in loco fuerit, quod posset provocare horrorem. Secundo, pertinet ad repraesentandum effectum gratiae, qua, sicut bono odore, Christus plenus fuit, secundum illud Gen. XXVII, *ecce, odor filii mei sicut odor agri pleni*; et a Christo derivatur ad fideles officio ministrorum, secundum illud II Cor. II, *odorem notitiae suae spargit per nos in omni loco.* Et ideo, undique thurificato altari, per quod Christus designatur, thurificantur omnes per ordinem.

Ad tertium dicendum quod sacerdos in celebratione Missae utitur crucesignatione ad exprimendam passionem Christi, quae ad crucem est terminata. Est autem passio Christi quibusdam quasi gradibus peracta. Nam primo fuit Christi traditio, quae facta est a Deo, a Iuda, et a Iudaeis. Quod significat trina crucesignatio super illa verba, *haec dona, haec munera, haec sancta sacrificia illibata.*

Secundo fuit Christi venditio. Est autem venditus sacerdotibus, Scribis et Pharisaeis. Ad quod significandum fit iterum trina crucesignatio super illa verba, *benedictam, adscriptam, ratam.* Vel ad ostendendum pretium venditionis, scilicet triginta denarios. Additur autem et duplex super illa verba, *ut nobis corpus et sanguis,* etc.,

To the second it must be said that we do not use incensation as a ceremonial precept of the law, but as a statute of the Church. Whence we do not use it in the same way as it was commanded in the Old Law. Yet it pertains to two things. First of all, to the reverence of this sacrament, namely so that, if there were any trace of a bad odor bodily in the place, which could provoke disgust, it might be dispelled through a good odor. Second, it pertains to the representation of the effect of grace, of which, as of a good odor, Christ was full, according to Genesis 27:27: *Behold, the odor of my Son as the odor of a full field*; and from Christ it is derived unto the faithful by the office of the ministers, according to 2 Corinthians 2:14: *He spread the odor of his renown through us in every place*. And thus, once the altar has been incensed everywhere, through which altar Christ is designated, all are incensed according to their order.

To the third it must be said that the priest in the celebration of the Mass uses the sign of the cross to express the Passion of Christ, which was terminated upon the cross. Yet the Passion of Christ was enacted through certain, as it were, steps. For first was the handing over of Christ, which was done by God, by Judas, and by the Jews. Which the triple sign of the cross signifies, at the words *haec dona, haec munera, haec sancta sacrificia illibata*.

Second was the selling of Christ. Yet he was sold to the priests, to the scribes, and to the Pharisees. To signify this, again there is made a triple sign of the cross, at the words *benedictam, adscriptam, ratam*. Or to show the price of the sale, namely thirty denarii. Yet there is added also a double sign of the cross at the words *ut*

ad designandam personam Iudae venditoris et Christi
venditi.

Tertio autem fuit praesignatio passionis Christi facta in
cena. Ad quod designandum, fiunt tertio duae cruces,
una in consecratione corporis, alia in consecratione
sanguinis, ubi utrobique dicitur benedixit.

Quarto autem fuit ipsa passio Christi. Unde, ad repraesentandum quinque plagas, fit quarto quintuplex crucesignatio super illa verba, *hostiam puram, hostiam sanctam,
hostiam immaculatam, panem sanctum vitae aeternae, et
calicem salutis perpetuae.*

Quinto, repraesentatur extensio corporis, et effusio sanguinis, et fructus passionis, per trinam crucesignationem
quae fit super illis verbis, *corpus et sanguinem sumpserimus,
omni benedictione* et cetera.

Sexto, repraesentatur triplex oratio quam fecit in cruce,
unam pro persecutoribus, cum dixit, *pater, ignosce illis*;
secundam pro liberatione a morte, cum dixit, *Deus, Deus
meus, ut quid dereliquisti me?* Tertia pertinet ad adeptio-
nem gloriae, cum dixit, *pater, in manus tuas commendo
spiritum meum.* Et ad hoc significandum, fit trina crucesignatio super illa verba, *sanctificas, vivificas, benedicis,*
et cetera.

Septimo, repraesentantur tres horae quibus pependit
in cruce, scilicet a sexta hora usque ad nonam. Et ad

nobis corpus et sanguis, etc., to designate the person of
Judas the seller and of Christ the sold.

Yet third there was the presignification of the Passion
of Christ made at the supper. To designate this, third,
two crosses are made, one at the consecration of the
body, the other at the consecration of the blood, both
times where the word *benedixit* is said.

Yet fourth there was the Passion of Christ itself. Whence,
to represent the five wounds, fourth, there is made a
fivefold sign of the cross at the words *hostiam puram,
hostiam sanctam, hostiam immaculatam, panem sanctum
vitae aeternae, et calicem salutis perpetuae.*

Fifth, there is represented the stretching of his body,
and the pouring out of his blood, and the fruit of the
Passion, through the triple sign of the cross that is
made over the words *corpus et sanguinem sumpserimus,
omni benedictione*, etc.

Sixth, there is represented the threefold prayer that he
made upon the cross, one for his persecutors, when he
said, *Father, forgive them* (Luke 23:34); second for liberation from death, when he said, *My God, my God, why
have you forsaken me?* (Matt 27:46); the third pertains
to the obtaining of glory, when he said, *Father, into your
hands I commend my spirit* (Luke 23:46). And to signify
this, a triple sign of the cross is made over the words
sanctificas, vivificas, benedicis, etc.

Seventh, there are represented the three hours during
which he hung upon the cross, namely from the sixth
hour until the ninth. And to signify this, again there is

hoc significandum, fit iterum trina crucesignatio ad illa verba, *per ipsum, et cum ipso, et in ipso*.

Octavo autem, repraesentatur separatio animae a corpore, per duas cruces subsequentes extra calicem factas.

Nono autem, repraesentatur resurrectio tertia die facta, per tres cruces quae fiunt ad illa verba, *pax domini sit semper vobiscum*.

Potest autem brevius dici quod consecratio huius sacramenti, et acceptio sacrificii, et fructus eius, procedit ex virtute crucis Christi. Et ideo, ubicumque fit mentio de aliquo horum, sacerdos crucesignatione utitur.

Ad quartum dicendum quod sacerdos post consecrationem non utitur crucesignatione ad benedicendum et consecrandum, sed solum ad commemorandum virtutem crucis et modum passionis Christi, ut ex dictis patet.

Ad quintum dicendum quod ea quae sacerdos in Missa facit, non sunt ridiculosae gesticulationes, fiunt enim ad aliquid repraesentandum. Quod enim sacerdos brachia extendit post consecrationem, significat extensionem brachiorum Christi in cruce. Levat etiam manus orando, ad designandum quod oratio eius pro populo dirigitur ad Deum, secundum illud Thren. III, *levemus corda nostra cum manibus ad Deum in caelum*. Et Exod. XVII dicitur quod, *cum levaret Moyses manus, vincebat Israel*. Quod

made a triple sign of the cross, at the words *Per ipsum, et cum ipso, et in ipso*.

Yet eighth, there is represented the separation of soul from body, through the two subsequent crosses made over the chalice.

Yet ninth, there is represented the Resurrection done on the third day, through the three crosses that are made at the words *Pax domini sit semper vobiscum*.

It can be said, in short, that the consecration of this sacrament, and the reception of the sacrifice, of its fruit, proceed from the power of the cross of Christ. And thus, every time that mention is made of any of these, the priest uses the sign of the cross.

To the fourth it must be said that the priest, after the consecration, does not use the sign of the cross to bless and consecrate, but only to commemorate the power of the cross and the mode of the Passion of Christ, as is clear from what has been said.

To the fifth it must be said that those things that the priest does in the Mass are not ridiculous gesticulations, for they are done to represent something. For that the priest extends his arms after the consecration, signifies the extension of the arms of Christ on the cross. He also lifts up his hands when praying, to designate that his prayer for the people is directed to God, according to Lamentations 3:41: *Let us lift up our hearts with our hands to God in heaven*. And Exodus 17:11 says that, *When Moses would lift up his hands, Israel would be conquering*. Yet that he joins his hands together and bows down,

autem manus interdum iungit, et inclinat se, suppliciter et humiliter orans, designat humilitatem et obedientiam Christi, ex qua passus est. Digitos autem iungit post consecrationem, scilicet pollicem cum indice, quibus corpus Christi consecratum tetigerat, ut, si qua particula digitis adhaeserat, non dispergatur. Quod pertinet ad reverentiam sacramenti.

Ad sextum dicendum quod quinquies se sacerdos vertit ad populum, ad designandum quod dominus die resurrectionis quinquies se manifestavit, ut supra dictum est in tractatu de resurrectione Christi. Salutat autem septies populum, scilicet quinque vicibus quando se convertit ad populum, et bis quando se non convertit, scilicet ante praefationem cum dicit, *dominus vobiscum*, et cum dicit, *pax domini sit semper vobiscum*, ad designandum septiformem gratiam spiritus sancti. Episcopus autem celebrans in festis in prima salutatione dicit, *pax vobis*, quod post resurrectionem dixit dominus, cuius personam repraesentat episcopus praecipue.

Ad septimum dicendum quod fractio hostiae tria significat, primo quidem, ipsam divisionem corporis Christi, quae facta est in passione; secundo, distinctionem corporis mystici secundum diversos status; tertio, distributionem gratiarum procedentium ex passione Christi, ut Dionysius dicit, III cap. Eccles. Hier. Unde talis fractio non inducit divisionem Christi.

praying submissively and humbly, designates the humility and obedience of Christ, out of which he suffered.
Yet he joins his digits after the consecration, namely
his thumb and index finger, with which he had touched
the consecrated body of Christ, so that, if any particle
should have stuck to his fingers, it would not be lost.
Which pertains to reverence for the sacrament.

To the sixth it must be said that the priest turns around
to the people five times, to designate that the Lord manifested himself five times on the day of the Resurrection,
as was said above in the treatise on Christ's Resurrection
(*ST* IIIa, Q. 55, a. 3, obj. 3). Yet he greets the people
seven times, namely the five times when he turns himself around to the people, and the two when he does
not turn around, namely before the Preface when he
says, *Dominus vobiscum*, and when he says, *Pax Domini
sit semper vobiscum*, to designate the sevenfold grace of
the Holy Spirit. Yet a bishop celebrating on feast days,
at the first greeting, says, *Pax vobis*, which our Lord,
whose person the bishop especially represents, said
after the Resurrection.

To the seventh it must be said that the fraction of the
host signifies three things: first of all, the very division
of the body of Christ, which was made in the Passion;
second, the distinction of the mystical body according
to various states; third, the distribution of graces proceeding from the Passion of Christ, as Denys says in
Chapter 3 of the *Ecclesiastical Hierarchy*. Whence such a
fraction does not introduce division into Christ.

To the eighth it must be said that, as Pope Sergius
says, and as is had in the decretals (*De Consecratione*,

Ad octavum dicendum quod, sicut Sergius Papa dicit, et habetur in decretis, de Consecr., dist. II, *triforme est corpus domini. Pars oblata in calicem Missa corpus Christi quod iam resurrexit, demonstrat,* scilicet ipsum Christum, et beatam virginem, vel si qui alii sancti cum corporibus sunt in gloria. *Pars comesta ambulans adhuc super terram,* quia scilicet viventes in terra sacramento uniuntur; et passionibus conteruntur, sicut panis comestus atteritur dentibus. *Pars in altari usque ad finem Missae remanens est corpus Christi in sepulcro remanens, quia usque in finem saeculi corpora sanctorum in sepulcris erunt,* quorum tamen animae sunt vel in Purgatorio vel in caelo. Hic tamen ritus non servatur modo, ut scilicet una pars servetur usque in finem Missae. Manet tamen eadem significatio partium. Quam quidam metrice expresserunt, dicentes, *hostia dividitur in partes, tincta beatos plene, sicca notat vivos, servata sepultos.*

Quidam tamen dicunt quod pars in calicem Missa significat eos qui vivunt in hoc mundo; pars autem extra calicem servata significat plene beatos quantum ad animam et corpus; pars autem comesta significat ceteros.

Ad nonum dicendum quod per calicem duo possunt significari. Uno modo, ipsa passio, quae repraesentatur in hoc sacramento. Et secundum hoc, per partem in calicem missam significantur illi qui adhuc sunt participes passionum Christi. Alio modo, potest

Distinction 2), "The body of the Lord is triform. The
offered part put into the chalice refers to the body of
Christ which is already resurrected," namely Christ himself, and the blessed Virgin, or if there are any other
saints who are with their bodies in glory. "The part
consumed refers to the body of Christ still walking
upon the earth," namely because those living on earth
are united by the sacrament; and they are ground down
by the passions, like the bread eaten is ground by the
teeth. "The part still remaining on the altar until the end
of Mass is the body of Christ remaining in the tomb,
because the bodies of the saints shall be in their tombs
even until the end of the age," nevertheless whose souls
are either in Purgatory or in heaven. Nevertheless, this
rite is no longer observed, namely that one part should
be reserved until the end of Mass. Nevertheless, the
same signification of parts remains. Which indeed they
express by meter, saying, "The host is divided into parts:
The intincted stands for those fully blessed, the dry for
the living, the reserved for the buried."

Nevertheless some say that the part put into the chalice signifies those who live in this world; yet the part
reserved outside the chalice signifies those fully blessed
as regards both soul and body; yet the part consumed
signifies the rest.

To the ninth it must be said that two things are signified
through the chalice. In one way, the Passion itself, which
is represented in this sacrament. And according to this,
through the part put into the chalice there are signified
those who still are participants in the passions of Christ.
In another way, there can be signified the enjoyment of
the blessed, which is also prefigured in this sacrament.

significari fruitio beata, quae etiam in hoc sacramento praefiguratur. Et ideo illi quorum corpora iam sunt in plena beatitudine, significantur per partem in calicem missam. Et est notandum quod pars in calicem missa non debet populo dari in supplementum communionis, quia panem intinctum non porrexit Christus nisi Iudae proditori.

Ad decimum dicendum quod vinum, ratione suae humiditatis, est ablutivum. Et ideo sumitur post perceptionem huius sacramenti, ad abluendum os, ne aliquae reliquiae remaneant, quod pertinet ad reverentiam sacramenti. Unde extra, de Celebrat. Miss., cap. ex parte, *sacerdos vino os perfundere debet postquam totum percepit sacramentum, nisi cum eodem die Missam aliam debuerit celebrare, ne, si forte vinum perfusionis acciperet, celebrationem aliam impediret.* Et eadem ratione perfundit vino digitos quibus corpus Christi tetigerat.

Ad undecimum dicendum quod veritas quantum ad aliquid debet respondere figurae, quia scilicet non debet pars hostiae consecratae de qua sacerdos et ministri, vel etiam populus communicat, in crastinum reservari. Unde, ut habetur de Consecr., dist. II, Clemens Papa statuit, *tanta holocausta in altario offerantur, quanta populo sufficere debeant. Quod si remanserint, in crastinum non reserventur, sed cum timore et tremore clericorum diligentia consumantur.* Quia tamen hoc sacramentum quotidie sumendum est, non autem agnus paschalis quotidie sumebatur; ideo oportet alias hostias consecratas pro infirmis conservare. Unde in eadem distinctione legitur,

And thus those whose bodies are already in full beatitude are signified through the part put into the chalice. And it must be noted that the part put into the chalice ought not to be given to the people as a supplement to communion, because Christ did not extend the intincted bread to anyone but Judas the betrayer.

To the tenth it must be said that wine, by reason of its humidity, is cleansing. And thus it is taken after the reception of this sacrament, to cleanse the mouth, lest any traces should remain, which pertains to reverence for the sacrament. Whence (*Extra, De Celebratione missae*, chap. *Ex parte*), "The priest ought to wet his mouth with wine after he has received the whole sacrament, except when he will have to celebrate another Mass on the same day, lest, if perhaps he were to receive wine for the ablutions, it would impede another celebration." And for the same reason he wets his fingers with wine, with which fingers he had touched the body of Christ.

To the eleventh it must be said that the truth ought to correspond to the figure in some respect, namely because the part of the consecrated host from which the priest and the ministers, or even the people, communicate, should not be reserved until the next day. Whence, as is had in *De Consecratione*, Distinction 2, Pope Clement commanded, "Let so many holocausts be offered upon the altar, as ought to suffice for the people. But if any should remain, let them not be reserved until the next day, but with fear and trembling let them be consumed by the diligence of the clerics." Nevertheless, because this sacrament must be received daily, yet the paschal lamb was not received daily; thus it is necessary to conserve other consecrated hosts for the sick. Whence in the same distinction, we read,

presbyter Eucharistiam semper habeat paratam, ut, quando
quis infirmatus fuerit, statim eum communicet, ne sine com-
munione moriatur.

Ad duodecimum dicendum quod in solemni celebratione
Missae plures debent adesse. Unde Soter Papa dicit, ut
habetur de Consecr., dist. I, *hoc quoque statutum est, ut*
nullus presbyterorum Missarum solemnia celebrare prae-
sumat, nisi, duobus praesentibus sibique respondentibus,
ipse tertius habeatur, quia, cum pluraliter ab eo dicitur,
dominus vobiscum, et illud in secretis, orate pro me, apertis-
sime convenit ut ipsi respondeatur salutationi. Unde et, ad
maiorem solemnitatem, ibidem statutum legitur quod
episcopus cum pluribus Missarum solemnia peragat. In
Missis tamen privatis sufficit unum habere ministrum,
qui gerit personam totius populi Catholici, ex cuius
persona sacerdoti pluraliter respondet.

"Let the presbyter always have the Eucharist prepared, so that, when anyone should be sick, he can communicate him at once, lest he should die without communion."

To the twelfth it must be said that in the solemn celebration of the Mass, many people ought to be present. Whence Pope Soter says, in *De Consecratione*, Distinction 1, "This also is commanded, that no one among the presbyters should presume to celebrate the solemnities of Masses, unless, with two present to respond to him, he should be considered the third, because, when there is spoken plurally by him, *Dominus vobiscum*, and in the secrets, *Orate pro me*, it is most clearly appropriate for responding to his greeting." Whence also, for greater solemnity, in the same place it is commanded that a bishop should perform the solemnities of Masses with many people. Nevertheless, in private Masses it suffices to have one minister, who bears the person of the whole Catholic people, in whose person he responds plurally to the priest.

APPENDIX 2

Diagrams

DIAGRAM 1: *Divisio Missae* in the *Sentences* (*In IV Sent.*, d. 8, ex.)

PRAYER	**Preparation** (preparation of the people for prayer)	**Introit** (preparation through devotion)		
		Kyrie (preparation through humility)		
		Gloria (preparation through right intention)		
	Collect (prayer to God for the people)			
CELEBRATION ITSELF	**Instruction** (through the word of God)	**Old Testament Readings** (ministry of prefiguration)		
		Epistle (ministry of manifest truth)		
		Gradual (advancement of virtues)		
		Alleluia (exultation from hope of eternal things) / **Tract** (exile of present misery)		
		Gospel (ministry of authority)		
		Credo (confession of faith)		
	Oblation	**Offertory Antiphon** (exultation of those offering)		
		Oblation Itself (offering of the matter to be consecrated)		
		Secret (prayer for the acceptance of the offering)		
	Consummation	**Preface** (preparation for the sacrament)	**Preface Dialogue** (arousal of the people to praise)	
			Preface Itself (prayer for the acceptance of praise)	
			Sanctus (praise itself)	
		Canon (completion of the sacrament)	**Te Igitur** (*sacramentum tantum*—blessing of the Oblation)	
			Memento of the Living (*sacramentum tantum*—commemoration of those for whose benefit it is offered)	
			Communicantes (*sacramentum tantum*—commemoration of those in whose reverence it is offered)	
			Hanc Igitur (*sacramentum tantum*—conclusion of what is sought)	
			Quam Oblationem (*res et sacramentum*—imploring of the power of God who will consecrate)	
			Qui Pridie (*res et sacramentum*—consecration itself)	
			Unde et Memores (*res et sacramentum*—commemoration of what was consecrated)	
			Supra Quae (*res tantum*—prayer that the sacrament, the cause of grace, be accepted)	
			Supplices Te Rogamus (*res tantum*—prayer that the effect of grace be given)	
			Memento of the Dead (*res tantum*—prayer that the effect of glory be given to the dead)	
			Nobis Quoque (*res tantum*—prayer that the effect of glory be given to the living)	
			Final Doxology (completion of the Canon in Christ)	
		Reception (reception of the sacrament)	**Preparation** (preparation for the reception)	**Lord's Prayer** (common preparation—petition of the sacrament)
				Libera Nos (common preparation—expiation of those receiving)
				Pax (common preparation—fulfillment of peace): **Pax Domini** (beginning by the priest)
				Pax (common preparation—fulfillment of peace): **Agnus Dei** (completion by the choir)
				Domine Jesu Christe (special preparation of the priest himself)
			Reception Itself (reception of Holy Communion)	
THANKSGIVING	**Communion Antiphon** (remembrance of the benefit received)			
	Postcommunion (thanksgiving in prayer)			

DIAGRAM 2: *Divisio Missae* in the *Summa Theologiae* (*ST* IIIa, Q. 83, a. 4, c.)

PREPARATION				**Introit** (divine praise)
				Kyrie (commemoration of present misery)
				Gloria (commemoration of heavenly glory)
				Collect (prayer that the people be considered worthy of such great mysteries)
INSTRUCTION				**Old Testament Readings** (dispositive instruction by the lectors)
				Epistle (dispositive instruction by the subdeacon)
				Gradual (progress of life)
				Alleluia (spiritual exultation) / **Tract** (spiritual groaning)
				Gospel (perfect instruction by the deacon)
				Credo (assent to the doctrine of Christ)
CELEBRATION OF THE MYSTERY	**Oblation** (offering as sacrifice)			**Offertory Antiphon** (happy praise of those offering)
				Oblation Itself
				Secret (prayer that the offering be acceptable)
	Consecration (consecration as sacrament)			**Preface** (arousal of the people to devotion)
				Sanctus (devout praise of Christ's divinity and humanity)
		Canon		**Te Igitur** (commemoration of the universal Church and those set in high places)
				Memento of the Living (commemoration of those who offer or for whom it is offered)
				Communicantes (commemoration of the saints)
				Hanc Igitur (conclusion of the petition that the Oblation be salvific)
				Quam Oblationem (turn to the consecration itself—prayer for the effect of the consecration)
				Qui Pridie (performance of the consecration through the words of the Savior)
				Unde et Memores (excuse from presumption)
				Supra Quae (prayer that the completed sacrifice be acceptable)
				Supplices Te Rogamus (prayer for the effect of this sacrifice and sacrament for those receiving)
				Memento of the Dead (prayer for the effect of this sacrifice and sacrament for the dead who can no longer receive)
				Nobis Quoque (prayer for the effect of this sacrifice and sacrament for those priests offering)
	Reception (reception as sacrament)	**Preparation for Reception** (through prayer and through peace)		**Lord's Prayer** (preparation through common prayer for daily bread)
				Libera Nos (preparation through private prayer by the priest for the people)
				Agnus Dei (preparation through peace)
		Reception Itself		**Priest's Reception** (priest as partaker of divine things)
				People's Reception (priest as handing on divine things to others)
THANKS-GIVING				**Communion Antiphon** (rejoicing of the people for the reception of the mystery)
				Postcommunion (prayer of thanksgiving)

DIAGRAM 3: Speakers

PRIEST (words by which the people is immediately ordered to God)	**Publicly** (regarding the whole people)
	Secretly (regarding the priest's own office)
MINISTERS (words that are handed down from above through the ministry of others)	
CHOIR (words that pertain to the disposing of the people)	**Alone** (those that are consonant with reason)
	With Priest Intoning (those that exceed human reason, as though received from above)
	Before Ministers and Priest (preparatory for receiving divine things)
	After Ministers and Priest (caused by the reception of divine things)

DIAGRAM 4: Significations

CHRIST'S PASSION (represented in this sacrament)
DISPOSITION OF THE CHURCH (signified in this sacrament)
DEVOTION AND REVERENCE (due to this sacrament)

DIAGRAM 5: Theological Virtues

FAITH (*Credo in unum Deum*)
HOPE (*Gloria in excelsis Deo*)
CHARITY (*Pax Domini sit semper vobiscum*)

DIAGRAM 6: Languages

GREEK (*Kyrie eleison*)
HEBREW (*Alleluia, Sabaoth, Hosanna, Amen*)
LATIN (almost everything else)

Made in United States
North Haven, CT
27 May 2024

52987530R00119